D1458046

LITANIES AND OTHER PRAYERS

This volume follows the new Revised Common Lectionary. Where necessary, the materials of the first edition of *Litanies and Other Prayers* have been altered or replaced to accommodate the new readings. The three-year lectionary cycle remains unchanged: Year A begins in Advent 1992 and 1995; Year B in Advent 1993 and 1996; Year C in Advent 1994 and 1997.

Litanies
and
Other
Prayers

FOR THE REVISED
COMMON LECTIONARY

YEAR B

Phyllis Cole
Everett Tilson

ABINGDON PRESS
Nashville

LITANIES AND OTHER PRAYERS FOR
THE REVISED COMMON LECTIONARY:
Year B

Copyright © 1990, 1993 by Abingdon Press

Litanies and prayers in this book may be reprinted for use in the local church
worship service, provided the following copyright notice is included:

From *Litanies and Other Prayers for the Revised Common Lectionary, Year B,* by
Everett Tilson and Phyllis Cole. Copyright © 1990, 1993 by Abingdon Press.
Reprinted by permission.

All rights reserved.
Other than the use stated above, no part of this work may be reproduced or
transmitted in any form or by any means, electronic or mechanical, including
photocopying and recording, or by any information storage or retrieval
system, except as may be expressly permitted by the 1976 Copyright Act or in
writing from the publisher. Requests for permission should be addressed in
writing to Abingdon Press, 201 Eighth Avenue, South, Nashville, TN 37203.

All readings taken from *The Revised Common Lectionary* © 1992 Consultation
on Common Texts are used by permission.

This book is printed on recycled, acid-free paper.

Library of Congress Cataloging-in-Publication Data

Cole, Phyllis, 1962–
    Litanies and other prayers for the revised Common lectionary.
  Year B/Phyllis Cole, Everett Tilson.
      p.   cm.
    Order of authors reversed on previous ed.
    Includes index.
    ISBN 0-687-22120-X (alk. paper)
      1. Common lectionary (1992) 2. Church year. 3. Pastoral prayers.
  4. Litanies. I. Tilson, Everett. II. Title.
BV30.T555   1993
264'.13—dc20   92-47126
                                                                                          CIP

MANUFACTURED IN THE UNITED STATES OF AMERICA

To
Charles Everett Tilson,
my newest grandchild,
with much love and
great expectations

and

To
Ralph and Dortha Price Cole
and Warren and Jeanette Oberholtzer Smith,
my grandparents,
in appreciation of your light,
now as ever

Contents

Introduction

This project (of which this is the second volume) is serendipity's child. The two of us were asked to write the prayers and litanies for the inauguration of the new president of the Methodist Theological School. To begin, we launched a painstaking search for models. Not greatly encouraged by what we found, we decided to create our own, interweaving the themes and images of the biblical passages selected for the occasion. This dialogue with Scripture, undertaken on behalf of a seminary community at worship, soon turned frustration into excitement. Biblical and contemporary images and ideas came together in meaningful and expressive fashion. Later we were pleased by the response to our efforts. Yet we were even more gratified by the challenge and insight we experienced in the writing. We felt that we had found a pattern by which to compose liturgical materials for Sunday services as well as special occasions.

While one of us is ordained and the other not, our experience in the worship of the church has been more alike than different. Both of us first worshiped in small town or rural churches. There the lections for any given Sunday were those chosen by the minister, usually for reasons known to the minister alone. Few of these ministers consciously tried to establish a thematic unity between the scripture lessons and other elements of the service. While this failure was not unforgivable, our experience of worship would have been enriched if such unity had been achieved.

From the first century the Scriptures have played a unifying role in Christian worship, which follows the pattern of Jewish tradition. The Protestant emphasis on the primacy of the Word heightened this focus, as illustrated by the hymns of Isaac Watts and Charles Wesley. Watts' hymns were often little more than a deliberate rendering of the Psalms into the contemporary English idiom. Wesley's hymns, reflecting a more comprehensive and evangelical use of the Bible, were no less inspired by the Scriptures.

In the course of time, however, the influence of the Bible on hymns and other elements of the service faded. Eventually the doctrine of the priesthood of all believers yielded a growing enthusiasm for lay participation in worship. This development was accompanied by a decreasing dependence on Scripture for liturgical expression. The liturgical imagination, shaped by tradition, became increasingly captive to the inspiration of the moment. The assumption survived that the sermon should be intimately connected to the Scriptures, but the unity between other elements of the service and the Scripture readings suffered.

The ecumenical movement has prompted us to lament this loss, and it has led Protestantism to a rediscovery of the lectionary. This, in turn, has kindled a new awareness of the need for both the *conscious integration of all the elements of the service* and their *dynamic interaction with the Scriptures.* Many resources are available which suggest complementary lections, hymns, invocations, and benedictions, and in increasing numbers they are based on the lectionary.

We regret that fuller lay participation in worship has contributed to the misuse—or nonuse—of the lectionary, but we would be the last to recommend *less* lay participation. The sanctity of the common life kept the movement behind the Protestant Reformers from becoming a backward movement. The common life enabled them to connect the past to the present, giving new shape to the future and also to Christian liturgy. What we seek now is not less but *deeper* lay participation. We seek participation that is informed and enriched by symbolism born of the encounter between religious tradition and modern life.

The renewed emphasis on spiritual formation has encouraged such participation, but this development has been a mixed blessing. For some worshipers, it has had the unfortunate effect of turning the heart inward upon itself rather than upward to God and outward to the neighbor. And, instead of bringing individuals closer together, it has sometimes set them apart, baptizing the notion that interest in one's soul may rightfully become one's sole interest.

Theoretically, use of the lectionary should prevent such distortion of the gospel, since its readings have been chosen *by* the community *for* the community. Ironically, though, this recovery of "spirituality" has led many churches to a preoccupation with worship, just as it has led many individuals to a preoccupation with personal piety. Rather than turning the church outward to the world, it has sometimes turned the church inward upon itself.

When the reformation of liturgical life is not accompanied by the transformation of public life, spirituality becomes heresy. Authentic spirituality expresses itself not only in services of worship, but also in worshipful service. It may take root in the sanctuary, but it must bear fruit in the street. It may begin with individual reflection in church, but it will not end until it has produced corporate action in society.

In recent works on the lectionary, such social awareness has been most evident in the attention paid to inclusive language. They have especially addressed—and tried to redress—sexist language in the lections. Their recognition of the role language plays in reflecting and in shaping our beliefs and behavior has been critical for the church. And, fortunately, these efforts have persisted despite criticism from some church circles.

But sexism is not the only villain that divides the Christian community and the human family. Evil wears many other masks—racism, nationalism, classism, ageism, and handicappism, to mention only a few. To overcome these divisive forces, we can begin by reforming the words we use, but we must dig beneath those words to their underlying attitudes. Words that exclude and offend spring from hearts that fail to include and affirm. Their usage testifies to something far more serious than a failure of language. It witnesses to the failure of faith.

Our faithful worship of the Lord as the God of all creation obliges us to cut the cloth of human concern on the pattern of divine love. And that obligation calls us to search for words whose usage will break down the ugly walls that separate persons of different genders, ethnic groups, nationalities, income levels, ages, and physical abilities. It is not enough

11

merely to avoid language that degrades and abuses other human beings. We must, instead, seek to speak words that will embrace and honor them. Our language in worship must be as inclusive as that traditional invitation to Communion, which calls to the table all "ye that do truly and earnestly repent of your sins, and are in love and charity with your neighbors."

Christians often cite our Lord's summary of the Great Commandment in the Decalogue (Matt. 22:34-40) as the hallmark statement of Christian inclusiveness. Yet we sometimes fail to recognize that statement's Old Testament roots. Such neglect of the Old Testament has characterized much Christian practice in the use of the lectionary. Despite the inclusion of its readings in lectionaries through the ages, the Old Testament has long suffered from inadequate attention in Christian preaching and worship. This oversight might be understandable if the content of New Testament lections did not so heavily rely on Old Testament language and imagery, and if New Testament theology did not so essentially derive its categories and their import from those of the Old Testament. We must, therefore, make a conscious and constant effort to correct this imbalance. Our aim must not be simply to give the Old Testament *its* due. We must also hope to give the New Testament *its* due, by tracing its ideas and images to their source.

Experts in communication have long recognized the importance of clothing truth in appealing language. The current stress in biblical studies on the use of imagery can be traced to this recognition. But imagery, to be clarifying and persuasive, must not only be vivid; it must also be visual. The hearer must be able to see what the speaker says. For this to happen, speakers must put themselves in the position of hearers, just as hearers must be able to put themselves in the position of speakers. We shall consciously strive, therefore, for language that will enable the users of this volume to hear with their eyes.

This resource assumes an intimate connection not only between the Bible and worship but also between worship and vocation. Indeed, worship may be conceived as a bridge between the Bible and vocation, with traffic moving in both directions. For just as we have drawn on the biblical witness to find appropriate images for the prayers in this volume, we have so elaborated them as to amplify the tasks to which God calls us in our world.

On this point two objections will be raised. Some will object that we have been more specific than we should have been about the nature of these tasks. We would reply that the biblical writers articulate the divine call in quite concrete and very particular terms. Others will feel that we have been less specific than we should have been. We would respond that it would be most unbiblical of God to reveal more to worshipers through the written word than through the spoken word. To the degree that we achieve our goal for this project, direct communication will proceed from indirect communication. God will take our place as your partner in dialogue.

Our use of imagery in these prayers is not limited to that found in the assigned lections. Biblical images, like biblical themes, leap the boundaries of books and chapters or verses to engage one another in dialogue. This thoughtful play of imagination, so obviously at work in the writing of the Bible, has inspired us in our reading of the Bible. We offer this reminder so that you will not be surprised when we employ imagery from other passages of Scripture to illuminate our presentation of the lectionary themes.

We offer one final piece of advice for the effective use of this volume: alter these prayers in any way that will make them more fully your own—by changing the language for addressing deity, by deleting or adding or substituting paragraphs, by localizing the points of reference. While we are responsible for the form they take in this book, you are responsible for the form they will take in your worship.

LITANIES AND OTHER PRAYERS

Abbreviations

A	All
L	Leader
M	Men
P	People
W	Women

Advent Season

First Sunday of Advent

Lections: Isaiah 64:1-9; Psalm 80:1-7, 17-19; I Corinthians 1:3-9;
Mark 13:24-37

Call to Worship
L: Christ shall come, God's gift to the world:
P: That the desperate should find hope—
L: That the persecuted should find peace—
P: That the lonely should find love—
L: That the dejected should find joy.
A: O Christ of the world, your time is now! We wait, we
    watch, we wonder! Come!

Invocation. O God, in times past we looked for you in
heavenly eclipses. We listened for you in howling winds. We
learned of you in quaking mountains.

But now we know that you will be found among us. And
you will be seen not in the glitter of a mall but in a shelter for
the homeless. You will be heard not in the pitch of a
commercial but in the whimper of a child. You will come, not
clothed in the comforts of the privileged but swaddled in the
needs of the neglected.

Open our eyes that we might witness the appearance of the
angels. Open our ears that we might hear the testimony of
the shepherds. Open our hearts that we might ponder the
secrets of Mary. And open our mouths that we might shout
the good news of the coming of the Lord!

Litany
L: Gracious God, in the Exodus you led Israel from slavery
    into freedom—
P: And then your children afflicted you like harsh
    taskmasters.

15

L: With the patience of a parent you greeted their rebellions,

P: But they continued to test your love like suspicious orphans.

L: O Lord, we call ourselves the new Israel, but we act like your children of old;

P: We call you the Spirit of the living present, but we worship the idol of a long-dead past.

L: We proclaim that you will bring justice without the sword and replace all death with life,

P: But our wars and rumors of war consume our world with violence.

L: O God, rekindle our hope for freedom, and spark our desire for peace,

A: That all taskmasters may become your servants, and all orphans may find their home!

Prayer for One Voice. On this first Sunday of Advent, memories of Christmases past flood our souls. We recall the first time we heard the stories—the journey of Mary and Joseph, the praise of the shepherds, the music of the angels, and the lure of the star. These stories had an earthly ring, but they sounded a heavenly anthem. The words were spoken in human tongues, but they proclaimed a divine visitation. And like the shepherds, we praised you for revealing yourself in a manger.

Surprise us again, O Lord, as you surprised us in those days. Let this Christmas come to us, as that first Christmas came to the shepherds, and we will echo their song of thanksgiving in the name of Jesus.

We do not make this request as servants worthy of praise but as defendants deserving rebuke. We never weary of repeating the mistakes of our ancestors. When our prayers go unanswered, our eyes accuse not ourselves but you. And when our plans go awry, our hearts indict not our ambitious pride but your cold indifference. Yet we stand before you with confidence, O God, assured that you begin the search for us before we begin the search for you.

By this knowledge we are moved to humility. It pains us to

16

ponder the take-for-granted attitude with which we accept your compassion and embrace your promise. We have become as casual about the gift of Christ as we have about the gifts of Santa Claus. Deliver us from the temptation to let this Christmas be just another Christmas.

As we depart for Bethlehem, let us contemplate the one whom we shall meet there—not a doting grandparent bearing gifts for the spoiled but a helpless baby seeking succor from the sensitive. Let us not become so confident in our work of preparation that we close the door against the possibility of surprise, for you never enter our world without surprising us. Israel's leaders foresaw your appearance in clashing swords, but your invasion of earth is heralded only by the gurgle of an infant.

So we pray that, as we await your coming *this* year, we shall do so with hearts yielded and minds chastened. Prepare us for a holy surprise. If you arrive at some other hour than eleven o'clock or some other day than Sunday, let us hearken to the song of your annunciation. And if you appear not in our sanctuary but in a shelter for the homeless, let us hasten to the site of your visitation.

When you came into Nazareth of Galilee, it was not merely to comfort but also to command, not solely to bless but also to judge, not alone to serve but also to rule. Even so, Lord Jesus, enter our world again. Surprise us as only God can—that, through you, we may come to God as, in you, God comes to us.

Benediction. We journey toward Bethlehem, O God, where you will reveal the glory of heaven and the hope of earth. May the light of your glory brighten our path to the future, and may the brilliance of your hope beckon us to new beginnings.

Second Sunday of Advent

Lections: Isaiah 40:1-11; Psalm 85:1-2, 8-13; II Peter 3:8-15*a*; Mark 1:1-8

LITANIES AND OTHER PRAYERS

Call to Worship

L: This is the season of live memories.

P: Let us remember the life of the One whose birth we hail.

L: This is the season of new beginnings.

P: Let us begin our watch for the One whose grace we extol.

L: This is the season of great expectations.

P: Let us expect the summons of the One whose love we proclaim.

L: This is the season of glad celebrations.

A: "O come, let us adore him, Christ the Lord!"[1]

Invocation. Eternal God, who in Jesus Christ awakens our hope for a new heaven and a new earth, we approach you with troubled but expectant hearts. We are troubled by conflicts within, yet reassured by your promise of salvation for those who trust you. We are troubled by conflicts without, yet encouraged by your pledge of peace for those who follow you.

Take from us, O God, the fear that we are not your people, and make us messengers of the hope for peace on earth.

Litany

L: Comfort my people, says the Lord. Speak unto them words of deliverance.

P: God will break the chains of the bound.

L: Comfort my people, says the Lord. Speak unto them words of peace.

P: God will cast out the fears of the troubled.

L: Comfort my people, says the Lord. Speak unto them words of order.

P: God will hallow the cause of the righteous.

L: Comfort my people, says the Lord. Speak unto them words of assurance.

P: God will raise the eyes of the hopeless.

L: Comfort my people, says the Lord. Speak unto them words of blessing.

[1] From the hymn "O Come, All Ye Faithful" by John F. Wade.

P: "Lord, give us faith and strength the road to build,
To see the promise of the day fulfilled,
When war shall be no more, and strife shall cease
Upon the highway of the Prince of Peace."[2]
A: Then faith and hope will shake hands, and love and
justice will embrace.

Prayer for One Voice. Almighty and everlasting God, you have ordained every time as a time of preparation for the coming of Christ. Yet we need the challenge of Advent to prepare for his birth. As with gratitude we recall his coming to first-century Jewry, let us with joy anticipate his coming to twentieth-century Christendom.

Deliver us from the temptation to turn this Christmas into just another Christmas. The season's commonplaces—the hanging of the greens, the lighting of the candles, the singing of the carols, the giving of the fruit baskets—have all too often become a mindless routine, engaging our purses rather than our hearts, calling attention to our diligence rather than our devotion. Forgive us, O God, for allowing this holy day to become a mere holiday, for letting eternity's invasion of time become an occasion for time's corruption of eternity, for permitting your symbol of divine self-giving to become our sanction of human self-seeking.

Grant us penitent hearts, dear Lord, that we might become bearers as well as receivers of your comfort. Let us make common cause with those for whom Christ's coming turns bad news into good news: captives in a strange land, strangers in their native land, the neglected poor, the abandoned young, the forgotten elderly, the desperate lonely—all those who have fallen victim to humanity's *in*humanity. O Holy Comforter, as you break once again into our midst, make us channels of your consolation. Proclaim your healing word through our surrendered lips. Manifest your transforming presence through our yielded hearts. Work your gracious deeds through our outstretched hands.

---

[2] From the hymn "Heralds of Christ" by Laura S. Copenhauer.

19

As we travel again the road to Bethlehem, let us not forget that Golgotha is our destination. Keep ever before us the connection between the cradle and the cross, lest we mute the glory of Christ's coming and repeat the shame of his going. As we listen to the song of the angels, let us remember the message of Calvary. With an eye toward Jerusalem, let us march to Bethlehem, coming to the Lord as the Lord came to us.

Benediction. We have heard the prophet's words of consolation for the humble, and we have heard the Baptist's words of judgment for the haughty.

As with these ancient worthies we anticipate the Coming One, let us prepare for Christ's table-turning presence, as he comes to redeem the shame of the lowly and to reveal the sham of the lofty. Let us receive his righteous judgment, that we might bestow his gentle consolation.

Third Sunday of Advent

Lections: Isaiah 61:1-4, 8-11; Luke 1:47-55; I Thessalonians 5:16-24; John 1:6-8, 19-28

Call to Worship
L: O come, let us adore him—
P: Whose coming was announced by the prophets.
L: O come, let us adore him—
P: Whose message was proclaimed by the angels.
L: O come, let us adore him—
P: Whose glory was hailed by the shepherds.
A: O come, let us adore him, Christ the Lord.[3]

Invocation. We read, O Lord, of the people's surprise when you were born in Bethlehem. They had expected a display of power, but were confronted by a picture of humility. They had looked for a mighty ruler, but were greeted by a lowly baby.

Chasten our expectations of this Christmas with the realism of that first Christmas, so that when you come to us,

---

[3] From the hymn "O Come, All Ye Faithful."

20

surprise shall give way, now as then, to recognition, and we shall hail you as "Wonderful Counselor, Mighty God, Everlasting Father, Prince of Peace."

Litany

L: When the Anointed One comes, what shall we see?
P: The broken-hearted being consoled and captives going free.
A: Open our eyes, that we may see the presence of the Lord!
L: When the Anointed One comes, what shall we hear?
P: The afflicted being lifted up and mourners made glad.
A: Open our ears, that we may hear the presence of the Lord!
L: When the Anointed One comes, what shall we feel?
P: The oppressed being delivered and prisoners released.
A: Open our hearts, that we may feel the presence of the Lord!
L: When the Anointed One comes, what shall we say?
P: The just are being vindicated and prophets made welcome.
A: Open our mouths, that we may shout the presence of the Lord!

Prayer for One Voice. O Eternal God, we bow before you, our Creator, in awe and gratitude. The grandeur of your majesty overwhelms us. Yet we adore you even more for the constancy of your love.

You do not need us as we need you. Yet you seek us before we seek you. Indeed, it is *because* you seek us that we seek you at all. So it has been from the beginning of time. And so it shall be until the end of time. For this, dear Lord, we thank you.

Yet we come before you with mixed emotions. Guilt intrudes upon our gratitude, and we are moved to confession. Even though we know better, we insist on setting the terms for our relationship with you: we substitute our lineage for your love in drawing the boundaries of our community; we flatter those who praise us even though they may not praise you; and we recruit you in the service of our mission instead of enlisting ourselves in the service of your mission.

Deliver us from our double-mindedness, O God, that we may pursue you with the devotion of the shepherds, praise you with the song of the angels, and present you with a gift even greater than the gifts of the wise men—the gift of ourselves.

As we offer ourselves upon your altar, dear Lord, we do so for the sake of your mission and not ours. We are grateful for all those who bear your cross with us. They do not make the task easy, but they do make it easier. So we pray for the increase of laborers in your vineyard. May the coming of Immanuel so transform the members of Christ's body that you, through us, shall overcome evil with good: moving the well-fed to care for the ill-fed, the strong to rescue the weak, the devout to commune with the indifferent, the well to minister to the sick, the learned to teach the ignorant, the natives to accept the refugees and the haves to remember the have-nots.

O God, as we await the coming of Christ into the world, we pray for the courage to embrace his mission *in* the world.

Benediction. May the One born in Bethlehem—who joined divinity and humanity, love of God and labor for people— unite heaven and earth, in us as in him.

Fourth Sunday of Advent

Lections: II Samuel 7:1-11, 16; Psalm 89:1-4, 19-26; Romans 16:25-27; Luke 1:26-38

Call to Worship
L: We're marching to Bethlehem,
P: To ponder the promise of the prophet.
L: We're marching to Bethlehem,
P: To sing the carol of the angels.
L: We're marching to Bethlehem,

P: To greet the Savior of the world.
A: "Come and worship, come and worship,
  Worship Christ, the newborn King."[4]

Invocation. O God, never ready to heed our demands but ever ready to hear our pleas, prepare us for the scandal of your advent. Deliver us from the pride of the mighty. Let us not forget that the Son of the Most High was the child of the most low. Remind us, as we celebrate your birth, that we kneel not to adore the Lord of the mansion but to worship the Lord of the manger.

Litany
L: We lighted the first candle of Advent,
P: To signal our watch for the coming of Christ,
A: Who will expel the spirit of discontent and bring healing for the nations.
L: We lighted the second candle of Advent,
P: To signal our hope for the renewal of creation,
A: Which will reveal the image of God and restore harmony with nature.
L: We lighted the third candle of Advent,
P: To signal our faith in the triumph of justice,
A: Which will expose the folly of pride and magnify purity of heart.
L: Today we have lighted the last candle of Advent,
P: To signal our trust in the promise of God,
A: Who will establish the reign of love on earth and uphold it with righteousness for evermore.

Prayer for One Voice. Gracious God, from whom we receive the gift of life, in whom we learn the meaning of life and to whom we owe the glory of life, we praise your holy name. We praise you for Jesus, who embodied human life that we might embody divine life.

We remember the story of Jesus' birth. Deep darkness shrouded the world, yet the light shone in the darkness, and

---

[4] From "Angels, from the Realms of Glory" by James Montgomery.

23

the darkness did not overcome it. The violent did not abandon their weapons. The covetous did not surrender their ambitions. The wealthy did not share their possessions. The powerful did not honor their positions. The pious did not bother with their confessions. But your light, shining in the darkness, revealed the bankruptcy of violence, the futility of envy, the poverty of riches, the debauchery of power, and the hypocrisy of false piety.

We have seen your light, O Lord, yet we continue to walk in the shadows. We doubt that, in the nuclear age, a successful war can ever be waged, but we spend dollars for defense and pennies for peace. We recognize that, on an overcrowded planet, mass poverty threatens the rich and poor alike, but the gap between them widens and deepens. We realize that, in a world come of age, the divorce of religion from life would spell the death of religion, yet the link between divine worship and human service grows weak.

Of this betrayal of your will, we wish we could plead innocent. But we know that you know our guilt better than we. So we approach you with penitent hearts, seeking your illuminating presence. Let the light that shone in Bethlehem shine in our world. Let it burst into flames and consume the rage that pits us one against another.

O God, as we survey the world that awaits its savior, lift the scales from our eyes that we might behold the people for whom Christ became flesh. And take from us our hardness of heart, that we might see that, for them, *we* were born. As the Word became flesh *for* us, let the Word become flesh *through* us.

Benediction. Send us home, O God, in the assurance that the power of the Most High will overshadow us as it did Mary. Then, when your surprises burst upon us, we shall greet them as Mary did hers, in the spirit of faithful surrender, saying, "Behold, we are the servants of the Lord; let it be to us according to your will."[5]

---

[5] Inspired by Luke 1:38.

Christmas Season

Lections: Isaiah 9:2-7; Psalm 96; Titus 2:11-14; Luke 2:1-20

Call to Worship

L: A trumpet blares through the silent night!
    A new song heralds the coming light!
P: Let us sing the new song,
    Let us turn to the light,
    Let us build a new earth,
    Let us celebrate new life!
L: Let the sea's deep rumble make the sky tremble!
    Let the field's high chanting make the clouds dance!
A: Let us sing the new song,
    Let us turn to the light,
    Let us build a new earth,
    Let us celebrate new life!

Invocation. O Shepherd of the world's peoples, we are alone in our fields, keeping watch in the night. Heavy clouds cover us; prowling wolves shadow us. Dispatch a shaft of light from heaven to kiss our feet! Send an angelic choir to sing their hymn in our midst! Show us the way to Bethlehem, that we may witness this thing that has happened. And when all is made known, we shall return to our fields, glorifying and praising you for all we have seen and heard.

Litany

L: We dwell in a land that is filled with deep shadows,
P: And yet your light bursts upon us.
A: O Radiant Star, lead us to dawn. Hear the prayer of your people!
L: We dwell in a land that worships the night,
P: And yet you break its power.

A: O Radiant Star, lead us to morning. Hear the prayer of your people!

L: You hear the boot of each tramping warrior;

P: You see every garment rolled red in blood;

L: You hear the boast of each strutting ruler;

P: You see every knee knelt down in the mud.

A: O Radiant Star, lead us to daylight. Hear the prayer of your people!

L: We dwell in a land that is filled with deep shadows,

P: And yet you show us the way.

A: Rest over the place where our new life lay. Hear the prayer of your people!

Prayer for One Voice. O God of creation, you cause the heavens to be glad and the earth to rejoice. You inspire the seas to roar and the fields to exalt. At your approach all the trees of the wood sing for joy, for they know that you come as no other comes: you come as righteousness and truth.

You come as the God of creation, and you remain as the God of the chosen. Who are the chosen? They are the Marys and the Josephs who, when you come upon them, find that they cannot easily return to their own city; that their place in the world has been redefined; that they will receive new life not in a mighty house, not even in a humble inn, but in a wretched stable. Who are the chosen? They are the shepherds who, when your glory appears around them, discover that they can no longer regard their fields and their flocks in quite the same way; that their place in the world has been redefined; that their hope will lie not among the Caesars, as they had always been told, but among the animals.

Who are the chosen? O God, they are those who, hearing your song in the heavens, seek your presence on earth. They are those who, locating the child, locate their own new place in the world. They are those who recognize that your grace appears for the salvation of all.

We are your chosen ones, O God. We are no longer alone. Our place is no longer what it was. For unto us a child is born; unto us an heir is given.

To this wrinkled, crying baby we would give the world, but the child has already claimed it for you. To this little, wriggling one we would give our future, but the child has already laid it in your hands. What, then, is left to give but the song ringing new in our hearts:

> O come, Desire of nations, bind
> All peoples in one heart and mind;
> Bid envy, strife, and quarrels cease;
> Fill the whole world with heaven's peace.
> Rejoice! Rejoice!
> Emmanuel [has] come to thee, O Israel![6]

Benediction

L: We came with haste. We found Mary and Joseph keeping watch in the night, and the baby crying in a manger.

P: Glory to God in the highest, and peace to all on earth!

L: Now, as we return to our fields, we will not forget;

P: We will keep all these things with gladness, pondering them in our hearts.

First Sunday After Christmas

Lections: Isaiah 61:10–62:3; Psalm 148; Galatians 4:4-7; Luke 2:22-40

Call to Worship

L: The word comes forth from the mouth of God!
   A new name shatters Caesar's rod!

P: Let us hear our new name,
   Let us turn to the light,
   Let us build a new earth,
   Let us celebrate new life!

---

[6] From the hymn "O Come, O Come, Emmanuel."

L: Let Simeon lift God's children to heaven!
    Let Anna reveal the name God has given!
A: Let us hear our new name,
    Let us turn to the light,
    Let us build a new earth,
    Let us celebrate new life!

Invocation. O Comforter of the world's peoples, we tarry in your temple, awaiting a sign. You have long promised that those who hunger for righteousness shall not taste death before their deliverance. But death swaggers now outside our door, taunting us with each strike of the clock.

Redeem us, O God. Send your life into our midst; deliver your spirit into our hearts. Then we, once feeble, shall cry, "God, my mother!" We, once feeble, shall cry, "God, my father!" We, once feeble, will become your children; we, once feeble, will take your name.

Litany
L: Embrace the Child and bless your God,
P: For the works of God's hands are faithful and just.
L: They have set a star to hang in the sky;
P: With a blazing torch our God shall lead us.
L: They have sewn the world a garment of light;
P: With swaddling love our God shall clothe us.
L: For the Child's sake, let us not keep silent;
P: For the Child's sake, let us not find rest,
A: Until all God's earth is robed in brightness,
    Until all God's earth shall burn with life!

Prayer for One Voice. This very hour we give thanks to you, O God. For on this day we who have seen much with our eyes have seen *all* with our hearts. We who have seen the dusk of so many old days have seen the dawn of a new day.

We, O God, have seen our salvation.

We easily could have *not* seen. Not because of tired eyes, but because of weary spirits. Time violates the heart; the advance of years breeds the anxieties of age. Oh, to be children again! To be cradled in the arms of our fathers, to be

28

lifted by the arms of our mothers! To be strangers once again to our parents' world!

But our childhood has vanished. We have grown, becoming strangers to one another and to ourselves. We have grown, becoming wise in the ways of our parents' world and feigning ignorance of the ways of your world.

We were groping for your new world, O God. In some remote corner of our foolish hearts, we were hoping for your salvation—but *this* is not what we expected. You sent no armies of angels to fight our fights, no yellow-brick roads to show us the way, no earthquakes to topple our great walls of fear. No, to save us, you sent what we had lost: You sent the child into our hearts, and we lifted the child into our arms and blessed your name.

This child is only one of many born among us, only one of many you have called holy, only one of many we have seen. Yet this child, whom we have seen *with our hearts*, has brought joy to all the world.

Still, our joy is pierced with great sorrow, for this child shall not remain a child. Surely he shall grow and become strong; he shall be filled with the wisdom of the new world. But when the child enters *our* world—Savior, we shudder to know that we shall rob him of his youth; that we shall sacrifice him upon ungodly altars. "Unto us a child is born," yes; but unto whom is this child given? Into whose hands, O God, have you commended his spirit? Are they ours, Lord? Is it we who have received him, only to give him up for thirty pieces of silver?

O God, return Mary and Joseph and Jesus safely to their own city. Be with them; watch over the Child as the days pass, but slow Time's course. Help us to prepare for him, to make straight our ways! Help us, before the hour is late, to bless, not curse; to declare, not deny; to trust, not betray; to be reborn, not die. Help us, O Lord, to keep the child within us safe, lest we destroy the child you sent to save us.

Benediction

L: Servants of God, depart now in peace; prophets, go in power—

29

P: For we have seen salvation prepared by the merciful hand of God.

L: With Mary and Joseph ponder these things; with Anna and Simeon praise the Lord.

P: Let us grow and be strong, that we may find wisdom.

A: May God's hand and ours hold the hands of earth's children.

Second Sunday After Christmas

Lections: Jeremiah 31:7-14; Psalm 147:12-20; Ephesians 1:3-14; John 1:1-18

Call to Worship

L: God's word runs swiftly to the ends of the earth!
It carries glad tidings of creation's rebirth!

P: Let us enter the new age,
Let us turn to the light,
Let us build a new earth,
Let us celebrate new life!

L: We arrive in a garden where suffering shall fade!
Proclaim the goodness of all God has made!

A: Let us enter the new age,
Let us turn to the light,
Let us build a new earth,
Let us celebrate new life!

Invocation. In the beginning was your Glory. It covered the earth like a mist, hovering in the valleys and hiding the peaks of the mountains. It watered the gardens of the lands, bringing forth the grain, the wine, and the oil. It ran in the beds of the rivers, laughing over the stones and catching the happy tears of the sky.

The Glory was life, and Life came to dwell among us, but we have not received it. Now the valleys are sinking into the seas, and the mountains are toppling into the plains. The wheat is withering in the field, and the grapes are shriveling on the vine. The rivers are running dry, and, as laughter dies, the sky can cry no more.

O Lord, the world cannot live without you. Come among us as before. As it was in the beginning, let it be now: a world without end.

Litany

L: Shout, "Hosanna!" and sing, "Alleluia!" For the glory of the Lord has risen upon you.

P: We have seen the star in the East, and have come to worship the Lord.

L: Cast your eyes round about, and behold the coming together of people from all over the world: exiles from the West marching hand in hand with sages from the East—

P: For it is good in God's sight that we walk together.

L: The Lord has come to judge the people with righteousness and the poor with justice;

P: To defend the cause of the weak and give deliverance to the needy.

L: The Lord has come upon us like rain on the mown grass, like showers that water the earth—

P: To turn the abundance of the sea to our good and restore earth's treasures to the people.

L: The Lord reigns from sea to sea and from Bethlehem to the ends of the earth!

P: May the leaders of the West, like the sages of the East, lay their treasures at the Lord's feet,

A: That we may know the hope that is born; that we may behold the new world we are given!

Prayer for One Voice. Long have we been in exile, O Lord; long have we been lost from the land of our birth. By the rivers of strange cities, the cities of our enemies, we have sat down and wept, remembering that place where once we lived—a safe place where despair was a stranger. But now *we* are the strangers in a strange land, and mocking waters flow quietly by, undisturbed by our troubles.

Shall we sing the Lord's song in a foreign land? Shall we sing the Lord's song at our captors' command? O, but how temptation sometimes tears at us as we stand before those who have hurt us! How the words torture our throats! How we, with the psalmist exiled in Babylon, would spit at our tormentors, "Happy shall be the one who dashes your children against the rock!"* Yes, we would sometimes save ourselves, sometimes heal ourselves by meeting cruelty with cruelty, hatred with hatred, death with death!

But from the Child have we received, grace upon grace; from the Child has the world received, grace upon grace upon grace. We and the world have received our redemption; embracing the babe, we embrace our salvation. In the Child's presence we weep with our enemies—first for shame, then for joy—for, from Bethlehem and Babylon and beyond, the Lord has gathered us together.

Together we shall walk by brooks of water, in a straight path on which we shall not stumble, for the Child shall lead the way.

Together we shall sing aloud on the heights, in a lofty place from which we shall not fall, for the Child shall sit among us.

Together we shall feast on the fatted calf, at a table from which we shall not be barred, for the Child shall break the bread and pour the wine.

And together we shall bid the little children come unto us, these children who might have suffered our spite, for the Child shall play among them.

Together we shall be led back, O God, and of you we shall be born again.

Benediction
L: There is a people sent from God whose name is Hope.
P: And the people named Hope shall bear witness to the light; despair shall not overcome us.
L: There is a people sent from God whose name is Love.
P: And the people named Love shall bear witness to the light; hatred shall not overwhelm us.
L: There is a people sent from God whose name is Life.
P: And the people named Life shall bear witness to the light; death shall not overpower us.

---

* See Psalm 137:9.

Season After Epiphany

(See "Celebration of Special Occasions" for prayers for Epiphany Day.)

Baptism of the Lord
First Sunday After Epiphany

Lections: Genesis 1:1-5; Psalm 29; Acts 19:1-7; Mark 1:4-11

Call to Worship

L: In the beginning is the Voice, and the Voice of God thunders over the waters,

P: The Voice of God sounds over the deep, saying,

L: "Come to the Jordan, wade into the stream, for the Lord grants strength to those who are weary,

P: For the Lord God blesses the peoples with peace!"

L: O children of earth, step off the bank and into the waters,

P: And the clouds shall be rent by the light of heaven.

L: There shall be evening, and there shall be morning:

A: And we shall worship the One who declares this day good!

Invocation. O God, your voice can split the heavens, part the waters, divide night from day. It can flash forth fire, shake the wilderness, thunder over the storm. Yet your word so often is heard among us not in the tempest, but in the silence.

Speak to us, O God, and let us listen, that we might detect the whisper of a wing, the rustle of a feather. Let us listen, that we might glimpse the dove and hear the voice that Jesus heard, saying, "You are my beloved; with you I am well pleased."

Speak again to us, O Lord, for when you speak, it is done, and behold, it is very good.

Litany

L: O people of mine, I roar upon the oceans; I howl upon the winds. But to those whose hearts have grown dull, my roar is but a whimper; my howl is but a sigh.

33

P: Speak, O Lord, for your servants hear, and we turn to you for healing.

L: O people of mine, I tremble with the earth; I quake within the mountains. But to some, my trembling is tranquility; to some, my quaking is calm.

P: Speak, O Lord, for your servants hear, and we turn to you for healing.

L: O people of mine, I laugh in the fire, but you hear only the hissing of sap.

P: Speak, O Lord.

L: I kiss you with the breath of my wings, but you hear only the rushing of air.

P: Tell us, O Lord.

L: You hear and hear, but do not understand; you see and see, but never perceive. How long, my people? How long?

P: Take us out to the wilderness, God, and to the river Jordan. And in these days the Christ shall come; the heavens shall open and the Spirit descend. And then, O Lord, your servants shall hear, and turn to you for healing.

Prayer for One Voice. O God, your ear hears the songs of the universe before they are sung, the symphonies before they are played, the harmonies before they are sounded. As your voice hums the lyrics of the canticle you have composed, your ear tunes the strings of the lyre you have crafted. You are composer, conductor, musician, and music, and you have created us to read the score, to follow your direction, to sing to your accompaniment, to dance with the Word.

Thus we know you. Your voice has sung to us, and its song is familiar. It rises in the majesty, falls in the agony, rushes in the ecstasy, and rests in the serenity known by your creatures. Sometimes, when we hear the rise and the fall, the rush and the rest, we begin—despite ourselves—to hum along with you. You glory in the entrance of our voices, and you lead us in the concert of creation.

We strain to hear your Word, O God, and you strain to hear our word. If we yodel from the heights of joy, you echo our song. If we wail from the depths of despair, you join our lamentation. If our voices peal in exaltation, you ring with them. If our voices pause in expectation, you wait with them.

But sometimes we are not so faithful as you, Lord. We are tempted to sing solo, to disrupt the flow of the song, to refuse to sing altogether. We head out into the desert to chant with lonely voices to the sands, and, although we are met by their silence, we would rather sit alone among the shifting dunes than stand with the chorus upon the rock.

But even when our words are not your words and our ways are not your ways, even when isolation tempts us to destruction and exultation surrenders to lamentation, your voice sends out the Word into your world. It stands before the entrance to the tomb, it edges near the threshold of the void, and there it sings a love song to life. And, behold, life dances forth from the grave, leaping to the rhythms of the universe.

We praise you, O God, for making your Word the Word of life. For since the beginning your voice has promised, that "as the rain and the snow come down from heaven, and . . . water the earth, making it bring forth and sprout, giving seed to the sower and bread to the eater, so shall my word be that goes forth from my mouth; *it shall not return to me empty, but it shall accomplish that which I purpose, and prosper in the thing for which I sent it.*"[7]

Benediction. May God go with you as you depart into the desert, there to meet the temptations of the soul. May the Spirit lead you to an oasis where waters run deep and clouds rise high, and where the voice of heaven whispers in the cool of the trees.

Second Sunday After Epiphany

Lections: I Samuel 3:1-20; Psalm 139:1-6, 13-18; I Corinthians 6:12-20; John 1:43-51

---

[7] See Isaiah 55:10-11.

35

Call to Worship

L: Is your soul barren, and swallowed by thirst?

P: The fountain of God springs from desert sands.

L: Is your soul faint, and devoured by hunger?

P: The feast of God spreads from a few loaves and fishes.

L: Is your soul weary, and dreaming of sleep?

P: The voice of God bids the dead rise from their beds.

L: Is your soul homeless, and sheltered by fear?

P: The hand of God builds a home on the rock.

A: Let us lift up our hands! Let our lips praise God's name! For steadfast love is better than life, and heaven's power is greater than death!

Invocation. O Lord, your word is rare in these days; there is no frequent vision. Wickedness is wrapped around our ears. Indifference is caked upon our eyes.

So speak to us through our children, God. They will be able to hear you, for when a thundercloud rumbles, they know the voice is yours. Appear to us through our children, God. They will be able to see you, for when a clown cries, they know the tear is yours. Come to us through our children, God, and we shall not be able to keep from asking, "What was it that God told you?"

Then they shall unstop our ears and open our eyes. Then we will know that you are the Lord.

Litany

L: Children of mine, I call to you!

P: Here we are!

L: How do you know where you are? Your sight has grown dim; you see nothing but yourselves, you know nothing but your own ways.

P: We keep to our place.

L: But what of *my* place? O children of mine, I call to you!

P: Here we are!

L: While in the night you toss on your bed, your little ones remain in the temple of God. Their sight is keen; they see beyond, they visit other worlds.

P: But you call to them. You send *us* silence.

36

L: O children of mine, I call to *you!*

P: Here we are!

L: *You* are my temple. My Spirit is *within* you. So wait for me; my Word will come.

P: And, as our young ones see visions, our old ones shall dream dreams.

L: Children of mine, I call to you!

P: Speak, O God, for your servants hear.

Prayer for One Voice. O God of Hannah, mother of Samuel and woman of God, who so longed for a child that she could no longer pray in words, receive our prayer. Grant us peace. For like Hannah, we have been barren. We have hoped. We have labored. We have expected. We have trusted. But our hopes have faded, our labors have been lost, our expectations have fallen, our trust has been broken. Yes, Lord, we know Hannah well. Send us the peace that came to her, even before her discovery that she was with child.

O God of Eli, father of rebellious sons and priest of a rebellious people, who so longed for a word from the Lord that he would hearken even to a word from a child, receive our prayer. Grant us your light. For like Eli, we have been unseeing. We have wandered about in a darkness of our own making. We have stumbled upon the bricks and stones of our own laying. We have been terrified of strange sounds and retreated to our own beds. Yes, Lord, we know Eli well. Send us the presence that came to him through the words of the child of Hannah.

O God of Samuel, son of a barren woman and servant of the Lord, who so longed for the sight of you that he slept beside your lamp in the temple, receive our prayer. Grant us clarity of vision. For like Samuel, we have been confused. Voices shout, whisper, grumble at us from all sides. At the shouting we tremble, at the whispering we shiver, at the grumbling we shrink. Which voice is yours? Which one, ours? Which one, theirs? Which do we follow, which ignore? Yes, Lord, we know Samuel well. Send us the clear vision that came to him through the guidance of his blind friend Eli.

O God of Philip, man of Galilee, who so longed for Israel's

37

deliverance that he rushed to tell Nathanael of the Messiah's arrival, receive our prayer. Grant us courage. For like Philip and his friends, we have been anxious. Who should be our leader? Many would rule us, many would teach us, many would tempt us. But the rulers' domination concedes little freedom. The teachers' instruction yields little enlightenment. And the tempters' persuasion offers little satisfaction. Yes, Lord, we know Philip well. Send us the courage that came to him when he found where Christ was abiding.

O God, we are not our own. Our hearts are yours; fulfill them. Our hearts are yours; reassure them. Our hearts are yours; inspire them. Our hearts are yours; empower them. Transform them into your temples, and we will listen for your voice.

Benediction. Someday soon we will be standing by the side of the road when someone walks by. And behold, we will recognize in that person the presence of Christ. When we are asked to "come and see" where Christ is staying, let us go. Let us not hesitate, for there we are needed; let us not hesitate, for we too have need. Let us make haste to the God who dwells with our neighbor, and together we will discover what once was hidden.

Third Sunday After Epiphany

Lections: Jonah 3:1-5, 10; Psalm 62:5-12; I Corinthians 7:29-31; Mark 1:14-20

Call to Worship
L: We have heard a prophet's cry;
P: The appointed hour has come.
L: We have heard a prophet's cry;
P: The realm of heaven has entered our midst.
L: We have heard a prophet's cry;
P: Let us turn from our nets and follow the Lord.
L: We have heard a prophet's cry;
A: Let us set our hearts and hopes on God!

Invocation. We have heard it spoken that almighty power belongs to God, and that to God belongs steadfast love.

So, to this power we appeal; with this love we plead. We have floundered too long in shifting sands; we need a rock on which to stand. We have shivered too often through bone-chilling storms; we need a refuge where we might find warmth.

For you alone we wait, O Lord. To you alone we pray, our Rock and our Redeemer.

Litany

L: When God's Word comes upon the world, the world is never again the same. An old age ends, a new day begins.

P: So, young Jonah, why sit and sulk?

L: When I caught wind of the Word of the Lord, I tried to run away. Why should *I* go to a hostile people in a faraway place, to deliver a message from another land's God?

P: But you did go, and they believed and repented. So, young Jonah, why sit and sulk?

L: Why did God attend to *their* prayers? *They* were not God's people!

P: But *they* did not need three days in a fish before *they* arose to follow the Lord.

L: When God's Word comes upon the world, the world is never again the same.

P: So, old Zebedee, why sit and scowl?

L: When I caught sight of the Word of the Lord, I went on mending my nets. Why should *I* drop my home and my work to chase a carpenter's dream?

P: But James and John went; they believed and repented. So, old Zebedee, why sit and scowl?

L: Why did God have to appear to *them?* They left *me* behind!

P: *They* did not want to cast nets from a boat to catch the fish of Galilee.

A: God's Word has come again to the world. Let the old age end! Let the new day begin!

Prayer for One Voice. O God, whose breath inspires life and whose heart beats in the womb of the world, how unfeeling we are! We fear the touch of your breath for it stirs the winds of change. We are numb to the rhythm of your heart for it brings the pangs of birth. When we feel, we fear, and we grow numb to the world that is our home. When we feel, we fear, and we grow numb among the creatures who are our family.

Release us, O God, that we may receive your spirit. Place our finger on the pulse of life. Transform us, and we shall know a world transformed: the ordinary shall become unusual, the routine shall become miracle. The time for loving shall seem short, and we shall love more ardently. The time for hating shall seem long, and we shall hate less fervently. We who have loved and lost shall find; we who have hated and gained shall lose. The last shall be first, and the first shall be last.

Release us, O God, and unleash us to do the work of the kingdom. Bid us rise, and send us even to those places that we consider defiled, even to those persons we consider unclean. Show them, through us, that your love may purify. And show us, through *them,* that we, too, must be purified.

Some of us, no doubt, will try to run away from the mission on which you send us. Wanting *comfortable* missions and *safe* visions, among our own kind and in our own place, we will board a ship heading in the opposite direction from where you would have us go. But you are persistent, God. If we flee, you will follow; swallowing us up, you will swim us back to shore, there to have us start again, there to give us another chance.

Some others of us will, no doubt, ignore you from the first and go on sitting in our boat, mending our nets. We will be all wrapped up in the old ways, and quick with excuses. We have spent our lives catching our fish, and we have caught them according to our own custom. And yet, to show us a new way, you raise up a *carpenter* to teach us. Why should we trust? Why should we risk?

But the winds of change are blowing. You breathe on us, commanding us, like Jonah, to love without passing

40

judgment. You breathe on us, commanding us, like Zebedee, to change against our better judgment.

And, yes, the pangs of birth are pounding. The time is fulfilled, and the kingdom of heaven is at hand. We shall repent, Spirit, and, rising up in power, we shall lift Zebedee from his seat and carry him with us into the new age. If we have fear, we shall be born to courage; if we are numb, we shall awaken to awareness. Only let us *feel*, O God, and we shall care for this world that is our home. Only let us *feel*, and we shall love these creatures who are our family.

Benediction. Arrest us, O God. The time of preparation is now past. The time of expectation is now fulfilled. As the new world rides into our midst like a child on the shoulder of Christ, let us stop—and look—and listen. For the form of our old world shall pass away, and the newly born shall lead us.

Fourth Sunday After Epiphany

Lections: Deuteronomy 18:15-20; Psalm 111; I Corinthians 8:1-13; Mark 1:21-28

Call to Worship
L: The works of God endure forever!
P: Great are they, and greatly to be praised.
L: Our God is the God of quail and manna,
P: Our God is the God of the fiery pillar,
L: Our God is the God of the prophet's mountain,
P: Our God is the God of the promised land.
A: Faithful and just are the works of heaven! Come, let our praise endure forever! Come, let us sing to the Lord our God!

Invocation. O God, whose essence is greater than anything we can sense, know us. Know us not in the way that a fact is known, but in the way that we are known by a beloved.

Know us, O God, and we shall know you. In our neighbors we shall see you; in our neighbors we shall love you. We shall love and see and come to know that you are no idol whose life

41

must be manufactured for the many. Rather, you are the One God, through whose life the many are made, through whose life the many are made one.

Litany

L: If your ear strains for the Word of the Lord and yet is afraid of the sound of God's voice,

P: Have no fear, for the Lord God will speak from the mouth of a prophet.

L: If your eye longs for the sight of the Lord and yet cannot bear to behold God's presence,

P: Have no fear, for the Lord God will appear in the form of a neighbor.

L: God has sent to us a prophet:

P: Let us hear the Word, and burn like a bush that is not consumed!

L: God has lent to us a neighbor:

P: Let us see the Word, and shine like a lamp that cannot be hidden!

Prayer for One Voice

> Source and Sovereign, Rock and Cloud,
> Fortress, Fountain, Shelter, Light,
> Judge, Defender, Mercy, Might,
> Life whose life all life endowed:
> May the church at prayer recall that
> no single holy name
> but the truth behind them all
> is the God whom we proclaim.[8]

O God, we speak names for you, yet your name is unspeakable.

You *are* what we call you, yet you are beyond what mere words can say. You *are* what we know you to be, yet you are more than mere knowledge can comprehend.

---

[8] From the hymn "Source and Sovereign, Rock and Cloud" by Thomas H. Troeger. Copyright © 1987 by Thomas H. Troeger. Reprinted by permission of Oxford University Press, Inc.

But if your name is unspeakable, you are not unapproach-able. Indeed, you approach *us*, an event so unthinkable, so unimaginable that we refuse to see you. You enter our presence and teach us. And while we are astonished at your teaching with such authority, we still do not recognize you. *We* do not, but the demons within us do. The evil within us acknowledges you as the Holy One of God, and you banish it from your presence. And still we are only amazed that a simple carpenter should command such authority.

You are a burning bush, Lord, but you are more than a bush that burns. Open our eyes when we see the bush, so that we cannot help but take off our shoes. You are a commanding word, but you are more than a master teacher. Open our ears when we hear the word, so that we cannot help but take up our bed and walk.

O God, your name is unspeakable, but we call upon you. Though you are beyond what mere words can say, our words rise to you. Though you are more than mere knowledge can comprehend, our minds reach for you. And more than any words or any knowledge, our hearts search for you, for they, too, would cry out with a loud voice, "I know who you are, the Holy One of God!" They, too, would say to you, "You are the Christ!" For you are

> Word and Wisdom, Root and Vine,
> Shepherd, Savior, Servant, Lamb,
> Well and Water, Bread and Wine,
> Way who leads us to I AM:
> May the church at prayer recall that
> no single holy name
> but the truth behind them all
> is the God whom we proclaim.[9]

Benediction. Go now in the knowledge that you are known by God and that you may know God. Go in the assurance that what is known is not as important as *who* is known. And go in the confidence that *whoever* is known will be loved.

---

[9] Ibid.

Fifth Sunday After Epiphany

Lections: Isaiah 40:21-31; Psalm 147:1-11, 20c; I Corinthians 9:16-23; Mark 1:29-39

Call to Worship

L: If you cry the cry of the brokenhearted, your God shall hear and bind you up.

P: If we plead the plea of the outcast, our God shall hear and bring us in.

A: Let us rejoice, and bind up all wounds; let us rejoice, and bring all peoples in! For the world is the Lord's, and the fullness thereof, and we are God's people together!

Invocation. O God, who heals the brokenhearted and binds up their wounds, hear us, for we lie sick with a fever. We toss on our bed, tormented by the dreams of the night and tortured by the fantasies of the day. Do not pass us by, Lord, but enter this house; come to us, take us by the hand and lift us up, that we may minister to you and the family of God.

Litany

L: Have we no power, Lord? The day drives us like slaves, and the night gives us no rest.

P: Your power overcomes the mightiest arm. Lord, be our power.

L: Have we no hope, Lord? Our days escape more swiftly than the breath from our lips, and the sun seems always setting.

P: Your hope penetrates the deepest shadow. Lord, be our hope.

L: Have we no love, Lord? Our months are pregnant with emptiness, and loneliness is the child we bear.

P: Your love endures the greatest betrayal. Lord, be our love.

L: Have we no healing, Lord? Years build up our bodies that disease may tear them down, and our souls become the dwelling-place of demons.

44

P: Your healing transforms the foulest death. Lord, be our healing.

W: If we are enslaved, free us.

M: If we are restless, fulfill us.

A: You are our power.

W: If we are chasing the sun, follow us.

M: If we are lost in shadows, find us.

A: You are our hope.

W: If we are empty, fill us.

M: If we are alone, face us.

A: You are our love.

W: If we are broken, form us.

M: If we are sinful, forgive us.

A: You are our healing. You, O Lord, are our healer.

Prayer for One Voice. O God, how you humble us! How you redefine our definitions, rendering our words obsolete by the activity of your Word! How you turn our world upside down, showing the wisdom of our ways to be the folly of the ages! How you reveal our truths to be riddles, converting our answers into questions!

You are, indeed, the God of the psalmist. You, whom we claim to worship, are not impressed by the strength of a stallion or the might of a human arm. Yet we idolize the strong and the mighty among us, be they mortal or machine. We trust them to entertain and amuse us, guide and protect us. Their strength allows us to be weak; their might permits us to be meek. While we watch from the sidelines, their ambitions compete, struggling to the last gasp. We are impressed, and we are perplexed that you are not. We cannot understand why you would take pleasure in our love for you and one another.

If you are the God of the psalmist, then you are indeed the God of Paul, once named Saul. You are the God of the angry, zealous defender of religious tradition who could not tolerate new visions. You smote him as he rode his stallion down the Damascus road, waving a persecutor's sword in his mighty arm. You knocked him down, you shone a light into his blinded, impassioned soul, and you said, "Saul, you do not

45

know what you do." Your love for him set him in a new world and gave him a new name: Paul, become free, become slave to all. Paul, become Jew among Jews and Gentile among Gentiles. Paul, become weak among weak and strong among strong. Paul, become all things to all people, so that others might see the light, dismount their horse, and throw down their sword.

If you are the God of Paul, then you are indeed the God of Simon's mother-in-law. She was probably an aging widow, not highly regarded in her community or in her son-in-law's household. She was not strong, but ill; she was not mighty, but a woman in a man's world. Yet your Son, O God, did not pass her by. He touched her, and she became a woman healed, a woman freed; a woman who arose from her bed not to resume the ordinary way of doing things, but to *minister* unto others; a woman healed on the Sabbath, who arose to serve the Lord of the Sabbath.

Simon did not understand the reality that Jesus of Nazareth had brought to Capernaum. He chased after Jesus and interrupted his time of prayer to beg for more miracles. Lord, if you are the God of Simon, then you are our God, for we, too, fail to understand this kingdom that you have sent into our midst. Open our hearts, that we may perceive what is real, what is desirable, what is good. Show us again what strength is, and what might can do, if it is yours. Help us sing of it, as did the psalmist; to preach about it, as did the apostle; and to embody it, as did the disciple, who understood and served.

Benediction. God freely gives that we might freely live. Freely God becomes one with us that we might become one with God. Freely God becomes all things to all people, that all might come to God.

Now we go forth with necessity laid upon our shoulders. For, while we are free, we must become slaves to the purpose of heaven, that liberation may visit the peoples of earth.

Sixth Sunday After Epiphany
(If this is Last Sunday After Epiphany, see p. 54.)

Lections: II Kings 5:1-14; Psalm 30; I Corinthians 9:24-27; Mark 1:40-45

Call to Worship

L: If the fiend of fear darkens your step, if the demon of pride dogs your trail,

P: Retreat into the hiding place; God shall surround you with love.

L: If the frost of winter nips at your heels, if the chill of death sits on your bones,

P: Come unto the hiding place; God shall wrap you in deliverance.

A: Blessed are they who hide in the Lord, for nothing is hidden that shall not be revealed. Blessed are they who trust in the Lord, for they shall find refuge and strength.

Invocation. We are untouchables in our own home; we wander among our own people as lepers. Touch us, Lord, and we shall be healed.

We are exiles in our own land; we pass among our own people as strangers. Enter our exile, Lord, and we shall kneel.

We are outcasts in our own world; we dwell among our own people as outsiders. Cast your lot among us, Lord, and we shall follow.

Litany

L: Naaman commanded mighty armies but had no charge over his disease. The Syrian king reigned a mighty empire but could not rule his servant's sickness.

P: And when the scepter of the king held no sway, the word of the Lord was spoken by a slave, stolen from the land of Israel:

W: "Go to the prophet who dwells with my people!" she cried. "Go, and be made clean!"

M: Naaman scoffed, and the mighty king trembled, but the maidservant knew, and she had no fear.

L: So Naaman burdened his beasts with gold, and the king sent a letter to Israel's throne:

P: "I have sent you my servant," wrote the Syrian lord. "His skin is afflicted; heal him, and live!"

W: Naaman insisted, but the little king whined,

M: For he knew no magic to heal the sores.

L: Then Elisha the prophet heard this Syrian's story, this enemy unhelped by the power of kings,

P: And he sent the word of the Lord to the hero: "Wash in the Jordan, and you will be clean."

W: But the general was angry, his honor offended. Why should *he* bathe in *Israelite* waters, in waters that flowed down so brown with mud?

M: "Wash, and be clean!"

W: But Naaman would not.

M: "Wash, and be clean!"

W: But Naaman could not.

A: But the maidservant had known, had been without fear. And the Syrian swam in his enemy's waters, and, lo, the wounded was made whole.

Prayer for One Voice. O Lord, you are the Great Healer. You touch, you tend; you bathe, you bind up; you deaden pain, you awaken joy. Your touch is tender, your tending is careful; your bathing is thorough, your binding up is gentle; your deadening of pain is merciful, and your awakening of joy is continual. You nurse the broken, but even before you reach for us, *you have looked for us.* You have sought us, and you have seen us. That you, the Great Healer, are also the Great Seer—this may be the greatest miracle of all.

We are a talented people, Lord. We are given the capacity to make ourselves invisible, and some of us practice long and hard to develop that capacity. Over the years we fade into a transparent, ghost-like existence. We glide in and out of people's lives, brushing by them without being touched. We observe them without being seen. We eavesdrop on them without being heard. It is easier if we become invisible, Lord, because we fear being slapped down, we fear appearing foolish, we fear the penalty for speaking the truth.

We are also given the capacity for making other people invisible, and some of us work long and hard to develop *that* capacity. Over the years we sharpen our image at the expense of others. We become numb to their touch; we become blind to their presence; we become deaf to their cries.

It is easier if we make them invisible, Lord, because their need makes demands on our power, their pain witnesses in the midst of our pleasure, and their world mocks the security of our own.

Forgive us our fear, O Healer. It would have us hide from your touch, the touch that would restore us to personhood. Forgive us our pride. It would have us deny that *our* touch could restore personhood to others. Forgive us for clamoring for miracles wrought by *your* hand, when you have laid the power to work miracles in *our* hands.

Paul writes about "running the good race." Lord, if we have fallen on the track, we pray for strength to struggle up and start running again. If we run but trip those next to us, stop us and have us lift them up. As we run, keep our eyes fixed not on a prize of this world but on a treasure of your kingdom on earth. Yours is a treasure imperishable, a trophy sanctified. It is a laurel that rests on the head inquiring into the truth, the heart searching for your will, and the hand reaching to the neighbor.

Let us leprous ones run to kneel before you, O Seer who will see us, that we might rise to run for you, O Healer who will heal us.

Benediction. You who have been healed, go forth from this place and spread your joy; for "the blind receive their sight and the lame walk, lepers are cleansed and the deaf hear, and the dead are raised up, and the poor have good news preached to them."[10] Blessed are they who can rejoice and be glad!

Seventh Sunday After Epiphany
(*If this is Last Sunday After Epiphany, see. p. 54.*)

Lections: Isaiah 43:18-25; Psalm 41; II Corinthians 1:18-22; Mark 2:1-12

Call to Worship
L: Remember not the former things, nor consider the things of old;

---

[10] See Matthew 11:5.

P: For the Lord is doing a new thing! Do we not perceive it?

L: Let us not look back to Eden but take the way God carves through the wilderness.

P: Let us not yearn for the milk and honey of the Promised Land but drink the water God brings forth from the desert.

L: Let us not dwell on old Exodus stories, for a new Moses leads us to freedom;

A: And this Moses shall put God's law within us, and write it upon our hearts; and the Lord shall be our God, and we shall be God's people.[11]

Invocation. Pathmaker God, prepare the way that we should go; make straight your paths. Long we have burdened you with our pettiness; long we have wearied you with our sin. But now, as you set us upon the road you are blazing into the new age, you promise that you will not hold the old age against us.

You have formed us to follow you into your kingdom, O God. May your faithfulness to us inspire our devotion to you.

Litany

L: I was wounded, Lord; I could not so much as rise from my bed. Yet my friends would do nothing but soothe me with scorn.

P: They came, pretending to care, armed with empty words and hollow gestures. Then they left, fingering sin as the cause of my wound, and the wound as my punishment, and you, my tormentor.

L: Even my best friend, whom I charged with my life, fled from my pain, thought me unworthy of care.

P: But you, O God, were not far from my bed.

L: You raised me up, and shamed them.

P: Now the one who forsook me lies upon his own bed, and the others murmur there.

L: Let me go to them, Lord. And together let us gently lift him, and carry him into your presence, and lay him at your feet.

---

[11] Inspired by Jeremiah 31:33.

P: Let me go to them, for I know that you are faithful; I know that you hear the cry of the wounded.

L: Great is your faithfulness, O God, and great does your faithfulness make my faith.

P: Who shall separate us from your love? Shall tribulation, or distress, or persecution, or famine, or nakedness, or peril, or sword?

A: No, for in all these things we are more than conquerors through the power of your love![12]

Prayer for One Voice. Faithful God, we have never seen anything like you. You are the Promise, and you are the Keeper of the Promise. You are the sun sinking into a bath of color at the close of the day, and you are the orange dawn awakening us for another. You are the memory of last spring sustaining us through the long winter, and you are the warm thaw signaling a new beginning. You are the One who, to save a people hurling its no at your face, whispers the yes into its ear. You are the One who, to send a Savior to creation, delivers a baby unto the world.

No, we have never seen anything quite like you. But we *have* seen someone in your likeness. You have sent someone among us who is Faithfulness itself, and we have betrayed it. You have sent someone who is Forgiveness itself, and we have passed judgment on it. And in so doing we have betrayed you, and we have passed judgment on ourselves.

We have never seen anything like you, but we have seen *someone* like you. But we have driven him away, unable to bear the sight of him or the sound of his words. He walked into our midst proclaiming a new age, and *bringing* a new age, but we are comfortable with the old. Can it be that we do not really *want* to see anything like you, God? Can it be that we do not really want to hear your voice? If you are the Promise, the Promise that would change the world, can it be that we do not really want you to keep it? And if all your "promises find their yes in Christ," can it be that we do not really want the Christ to come?

---

[12] Taken from Romans 8:35, 37.

Lord, forgive us for exacting faithfulness from you but not from ourselves. And pardon us for claiming that forgiveness can flow from you and you alone. Send us people, O God, whose faithfulness will help us become faithful, whose forgiveness will help us forgive. Send us people, O God, who shout "Amen!" to your Promise. Send us people, O God, who can bring us paralytics of the spirit into the presence of the holy, where our resolve can be strengthened and our bodies renewed. Then shall the world be amazed and glorify your name.

Benediction. In the assurance of forgiveness, I say to you, rise, take up your bed and walk. Do not stand still, but leap for joy. Do not take one step and falter, but run ahead of the One who comes. For as surely as God is faithful, the Promise is here and shall be made known. And, upon being touched by that Promise, no one of us shall ever again be the same.

Eighth Sunday After Epiphany
(*If this is Last Sunday After Epiphany, see p. 54.*)

Lections: Hosea 2:14-20; Psalm 103:1-13, 22; II Corinthians 3:1-6; Mark 2:13-22

Call to Worship
L: Bless the Lord, O my soul; and all that is within me, bless God's holy name!
P: Bless my soul, O my Lord; and upon my heart so tenderly write your holy name!
L: Your name is mercy,
P: Your name is justice;
L: Your name is love,
P: And faithfulness!
A: Let us bare our hearts to heaven, that peace and life may there be written!

Invocation. Savior of the world, we walk through the valley of the shadow of death. You have promised to make of that valley a doorway to life. Behold, we stand at the door and knock; hear our voice and open, and we will come in.[13]

---
[13] Inspired by Revelation 3:20.

Litany

L: The day will come when we shall kneel and call our God "Beloved."

P: On that day we will smash our idols and forget their names, and then we shall remember the names of the beasts and the birds.

L: On that day God will snap our bows and scatter the pieces; God will splinter our spears and shatter our swords,

A: And war shall never more murder the land.

L: We will fix our hearts not on war but on peace;

P: We will pillow our heads not on weapons but dreams;

L: We will value our hands not as fists but as palms;

P: We will guard our homes not as foxes but lambs.

L: On that day when our God is "Beloved," the new covenant will reign on earth as in heaven.

P: Of its peace are we the priests;

L: Of its dreams are we the prophets;

P: Of its palms are we the stewards;

L: Of its lambs are we the shepherds.

A: Of that covenant Christ was the first, and of that covenant the Spirit is the last. It is written on the tablet of our hearts; may it be read by the soul, may it be known in the flesh.

Prayer for One Voice.

Beloved God, we seek you.
Beloved God, we need you.
Beloved God, we know you.
Lover of souls, we would know you better.

When we are trapped in our folly, you whisper in our ear the way to freedom. When we are unfaithful, you court us with tenderness and lure us back to a familiar place, a fertile place that once we shared. There you kneel with us and prepare the soil for a pleasant planting. As we sift the earth through trembling fingers and smell its moistness and feel its warmth, you set the vines for the vineyards of your people. Reminding us of the past that we lived with you in this place, you plant our hope for the future.

Lover of souls, we would know you better.

When we are most unmerciful, you are Mercy. When we are least gracious, you are Grace. You are slow to anger; you pluck the sins from our confessing tongues and hurl them as far away as the East is from the West. You abound in a steadfast love that towers like the heavens above the earth; you scoop from the ground the evils our hands have wrought and fling them into the clouds.

And soon thereafter it always rains, and a rainbow arches over the fields. The rain waters are our evil made pure. They baptize our vineyard with life, for you do not desire that we eat sour grapes, nor that our children's teeth be set on edge.[14]

Beloved God, we would know your name. Christen us.

Beloved God, we need your power. Possess us.

Beloved God, we seek your presence. Find us.

Benediction. O God, make us vessels worthy of the wine of the new covenant. Let us carry it across an earth drenched with blood, anointing the wounds of God's peoples and raising the cup to their feverish lips. For long has the covenant been promised to the world, and long shall its wine be poured out for many.

Transfiguration Sunday
Last Sunday After Epiphany

Lections: II Kings 2:1-12*a*; Psalm 50:1-6; II Corinthians 4:3-6; Mark 9:2-9

Call to Worship

L: Our God comes, and a summons is heard through all the earth.

P: Let us rise to greet our God with songs of great rejoicing.

L: Our God comes, and a devouring fire leads the way.

---

[14] Inspired by Jeremiah 31:29-30.

P: Let us dance around the blaze and be refined in its flames.

L: Our God comes, and a mighty wind roars round about.

P: Let us leap onto its wings and fly to heaven's door.

L: Our God comes, and the shining forth blots out the sun.

A: Let us kneel in silence before the light, for once we sat in darkness.

Invocation. O God, you are the One who, on the very first day of creation, declared, "Let there be light"; and there was light, and you saw that it was good. Ever since, your light has been within us, but the gods of this world have eclipsed it. We can no longer see the sun that you set above us to illumine our way.

Come to us, O Healer of Blindness, and shine your glory upon our hearts, that we might be your witnesses once again. If in this world we must be blind, let us be blinded by your presence.

Litany

L: O Lord, you take us to the mountaintop, but we are dizzied by the height.

P: You would show us who you are, but we are blinded by the brilliance of your garment.

L: You would have us know the importance of the present, but we are visited by prophets wearing mantles of the past.

P: You would teach us how to build your kingdom, but we are content merely to erect your shelter.

L: You would make clear your will for us, but we are overshadowed by a cloud.

P: You would speak to us and make things plain, but we are amazed by another voice rumbling from heaven.

L: O Lord, at your baptism the sun shone like your garment does now, and the prophet John laid his hands on your head. At your baptism something new was beginning, but we did not know what it was; something new was being said, but we could not hear the voice.

P: But now we hear, and the voice is saying, "This is my beloved Son; to this one you shall listen."

L: And though we still question in our hearts what this means,

P: We will follow you.

L: And though we descend the mountain fearing what mystery lies ahead,

P: We will trust you.

A: As surely as God lives, we will never leave you.

Prayer for One Voice. Lord, a prophet appeared in the wilderness, calling us to a baptism of repentance. And we went out to him, and we were baptized in the river Jordan, confessing our sin.

A man named Jesus also came. And when he waded from the water, we saw the heavens open and the sun stream through, but we thought only that the cloud cover had finally broken. And, too, it is said that a voice spoke from heaven, but we heard only a distant rumbling, like thunder rolling over the hills.

We remember that day, not because of the deep impression it made, but because this day has brought it to mind. Today we have seen and heard what then we did not see and hear. We have seen a man transfigured, and we have heard his name revealed. But with trembling we must confess: we understand little more this day than we did then.

We must also admit that the memory of our own baptism has faded. Its meaning has paled. For in our world "repentance for the forgiveness of sin" is a foreign language. "Pride in the pursuit of pleasure" is our native tongue.

Lead us up the high mountain, Lord, and transfigure us. At our baptism we pledged to you our souls, and we were reborn by the water. Now we pledge to you our very lives, that we may be reborn by the Spirit. We will hold nothing back, for nothing is ours to retain. At creation you made us in your image. Reshape us now in your likeness, for we have donned the masks of other gods. Our land is filled with them, and these we worship, the painted works of our own hands.[15]

---

[15] Inspired by Isaiah 2:8.

Clothe us in light, Lord, for we would be children of the light. Send to us your word, Lord, for we would be doers of the word. Lay on us your mantle, Lord, for we follow the One who wears the crown. Lord, we remember our baptism. May we receive our transfiguration.

Benediction. Lord, we have seen, but we are not convinced of the truth of our vision. Make it sure, and make us prophets of your presence, whether you stand on the pinnacle or the plain, in splendor or simplicity.

Lenten Season

Ash Wednesday

Lections: Joel 2:1-2, 12-17a; Psalm 51:1-17; II Corinthians 5:20b–6:2 (3-10 optional); Matthew 6:1-6, 16-21

Call to Worship

L: The trumpet of the Lord sounds, calling us to examine our souls,

P: For we have not only met temptation, we have felt its grip.

L: The trumpet of the Lord sounds, calling us to mend our ways,

P: For we have not only committed sin, we have felt its sting.

L: The trumpet of the Lord sounds, calling us to rend our hearts,

P: For we have not only witnessed forgiveness, we have felt its power.

A: O come, let us worship the Lord!

Invocation. Almighty and eternal God, you endow us with gifts worthy of creatures made in your image. Yet you do not abandon us when we use them for alien purposes. Not only do you forgive us when we come to you with penitent hearts, you pursue us with a love that will not let us stay away. O Lord, let us so mediate this love that we will cease from the abuse of your gifts and the distortion of your image.

Litany

L: Our Lord took the shortcut to the desert to prepare for the long journey to Calvary.[16]

P: Let *us* prepare, that we might commend ourselves as servants of the Lord.

L: If we have created obstacles by leaving it to others to take the risks of faith,

---

[16] See Matthew 4:1.

P: Blot out our transgressions, O God, and create in us a clean heart and a right spirit.

L: If we have created obstacles by leaving it to others to manifest the gifts of love,

P: Blot out our transgressions, O God.

L: If we have created obstacles by leaving it to others to display the marks of truth,

P: Blot out our transgressions, O God.

L: If we have created obstacles by leaving it to others to bear the fruits of the gospel,

P: Blot out our transgressions, O God.

L: If we have created obstacles by leaving it to others to carry the cross of Christ,

A: Blot out our transgressions, O God, and create in us a clean heart and a right spirit. Take us with you into the desert, that we might prepare for the journey to Calvary.

Prayer for One Voice. O God, from whom we are ever prone to stray but who always remains close enough to hear our cry for help, we approach you with a sense of shame and a sigh of relief. When we think of how little we have done with all you have given us, we are ashamed—ashamed of our deafness to your call to replenish the earth and tend it; to join them our brothers and sisters in making our planet safe for humanity; and to practice our piety to be seen of God rather than our neighbors.

Despite our shame, we are relieved—relieved that you have not acted on the reasons we have given you for forsaking us; that you have not abandoned your creation or your reliance on your creatures; and that people are demanding a form of worship that puts less emphasis on form and more emphasis on worship. So we are not only relieved but delighted to be able to greet still another Ash Wednesday as a people who are still alive, still loved, and still yours.

We thank you, O God, that we can always count on you to deal with us, not according to our sin, but according to your mercy. Not overlooking our bent to falsehood, you demand that we pursue the truth. Not discounting our inclination for folly, you offer us a diet of wisdom. Not disregarding our thirst for peace of mind, you dispense the joy of salvation only to right spirits and pure hearts.

We wish, O Lord, that you could count on us as we count on you. But you know our record of transgression too well for us not to come clean. We earnestly and truly repent of our sin, and are heartily sorry for our transgressions. Remove them as far from us as the East is from the West. And create in us a heart within which they will never again find a home.

This is the day of the Lord! O Lord, proclaim to the people the good news that your day is their day, too. Show us the stepping-stones, one by one, with which Jesus marked the road that leads to you—the Jesus who faced every trial with which we could be tested, but was upended by none of them; the Jesus who was tempted by every vice to which we are vulnerable, but was subdued by none of them; the Jesus who was treated as if he were below our contempt, but who died as one above our reproach. Forgive us, O God, for having buried his stepping-stones beneath our stumbling blocks. Create in us a clean heart and renew a right spirit within us, not only that we may walk in his shoes, but that we may add new stepping-stones to those he has already laid.

Benediction. Dear Lord, who calls not the well but the sick to repentance, anoint us to be agents of your healing ministry. Send us forth as heralds of the fasting to which your prophet Isaiah calls us—the fast that loosens the bonds of wickedness, frees the oppressed, feeds the hungry, houses the homeless and clothes the naked[17]—so that, when people ask, "Where are you, Lord?" you can answer, "Here I am."[18]

First Sunday in Lent

Lections: Genesis 9:8-17; Psalm 25:1-10; I Peter 3:18-22; Mark 1:9-15

---

[17] See Isaiah 58:6 f.
[18] Inspired by Isaiah 6:8.

Call to Worship

L: We have come together to praise our Maker.

P: But we have betrayed the purpose of the Lord.

L: The Lord is God of the Second Chance, and the Lord invites us into the divine presence.

P: But we have sinned against the Lord.

L: The Lord is God of the Second Chance, and the Lord grants us redemption from sin.

P: But our transgressions have estranged us from the Lord.

L: The Lord is God of the Second Chance, and the Lord offers us reconciliation through Christ.

A: We stand in awe of you, O Lord, who creates, redeems, and reconciles. Let us praise you with our lips and our lives.

Invocation. O God, who in creation fashions us in your image, who in Christ reveals to us your love, who through the Holy Spirit welcomes us into the fellowship of believers, we bow in gratitude before you. We constantly distort your image, but still you restore it. We daily betray your love, but still you extend it. We often disrupt the fellowship, but still you bless it.

Come unto us at this time and in this place, O Lord, that your image in us might be revealed, your love for us returned, and our fellowship in Christ renewed.

Litany

L: The Lord has been faithful, but we have been faithless.

P: Remember us, O Lord, not according to our transgressions, but according to your love.

L: The Lord has revealed to us the paths of truth, but we have strayed from those paths.

P: Yet if we turn to the Lord in repentance, the Lord may still turn to us in mercy.

L: "Blow the trumpet in Zion!"[19] The rainbow is in the clouds; the Lord remembers our covenant.

P: Forgive us, O God, and we will be faithful.

A: And we too will remember that our covenant is forever.

---

[19] See Joel 2:1.

Prayer for One Voice. O Lord and lover of us all, by whose power we stand and before whose goodness we bow, we praise you for your matchless patience. We have given you ample reason to turn away from us, but your face is turned ever toward us. Try as we may to make it on our own, you do not abandon us to our own devices. You come to us as a caring mother, wooing us home with open arms and challenging us with a love as persistent as it is pure. Even though we spurn you, you do not spurn us. And though our loyalty often wavers, your patience never wears thin.

We thank you, O God, for your patience. Not only does it overcome our anxiety; it exceeds your justice as well. If you dealt with us according to our just deserts, none of us could stand. Yet we address you in confidence and in hope, assured that your patience is a match even for our disobedience; assured that, while it may be late for our repentance, it is not too late for your forgiveness; and assured that, even though our love has let go of you, your love will never let go of us.

As we ponder this love, we are reminded of our calling to become its agents. This call has fallen on deaf ears and hard hearts. We have not so commended ourselves as your servants as to remove the obstacles in the way of our neighbors. We have strewn their path with so many obstacles that we leave them wondering just whose servants we really are. When adversity strikes, they are not surprised to hear from us cries of lament rather than hymns of fortitude. When opposition mounts, they are not surprised to see us fleeing the scene rather than standing our ground. But they are surprised, when we are afforded the chance to speak the truth in love, to find us willing to take the risk.

If we had given only our neighbors reason to be displeased, we would have ground for remorse. But in failing them, O Lord, we have also failed you. We have betrayed you, not only by the good deeds we could have done for our neighbors but did not. We have betrayed you also by the good deeds we did solely for their benefit: by the alms we gave to be noticed not by you but by them; by the prayers we mouthed to be heard not by you but by them; and by the fasting we endured to be witnessed not by you but by them.

For our sin, whether expressed in acts of omission or commission, we ask your forgiveness, O Lord. Give us a penitent heart, and fill us with an obedient spirit, that we might discern and do your will. Restore to us the joy of our salvation, that before our neighbors we might place not stumbling-blocks but stepping-stones; and that we might, on the streets as in the sanctuary, become the agents of your mission.

O God, bring us and our neighbors together in a fellowship so compelling that we will proclaim your gospel as Jesus proclaimed it to the Galileans, saying, "The time is fulfilled, and the reign of God is at hand; repent, and believe in the gospel."

Benediction. As we go forth into the world, let our worship be to us as the rainbow was to Noah: a reminder of your covenant with us, that we might be instruments of your blessing.

Second Sunday in Lent

Lections: Genesis 17:1-7, 15-16; Psalm 22:23-31; Romans 4:13-25; Mark 8:31-38

Call to Worship
L: The Lord entered into covenant with Abraham and Sarah,
P: And not only with them, but also with us.
L: At times they doubted because of their age,
P: And at times we doubt because of our sin.
L: But the Lord is God, and the covenant is everlasting.
A: O come, let us celebrate our covenant with the Lord!

Invocation. O God, who creates all persons to bear your image, all minds to discern your purpose, all hearts to reveal your love, and all wills to heed your summons, we marvel at the grace with which you surround us. You love us with a love we do not deserve. Yet we do not love you with the love you do deserve. Teach us this day, O Lord, to love you as you love us. Open our eyes, that we might behold your image in us, discern your will for us, and heed your summons to us, not only in our worship but also in our work.

Litany

L: I was walking down Main Street when an alcoholic cried, "I have no family. I am all alone."

P: You are not alone, but a member of God's family and ours.

L: I was leaving the grocery when a child wailed, "I have no food. I am all alone."

P: You are not alone, but a member of God's family and ours.

L: I was stopped at a red light when a youth screamed, "I have no home. I am all alone."

P: You are not alone, but a member of God's family and ours.

L: I was entering the church when a stranger confessed, "I have no friends. I am all alone."

P: You are not alone, but a member of God's family and ours.

L: I was visiting a nursing home when a grandmother confided, "I have no hope. I am all alone."

P: You are not alone, but a member of God's family and ours.

A: When your people *feel* alone, help us to make sure, O God, that they not *be* alone.

Prayer for One Voice. O God of Abraham and Sarah, Isaac and Rebekah, Jacob and Rachel, with deep humility we recall your covenant with our ancestors. No matter how much their faith wavered—and they all had moments of doubt and uncertainty—*you* remained ever faithful. No matter how often they broke covenant with you, *you* always kept covenant with them. As it was with them, so it is with us. The covenant is alive and well, not because of us but because of you. So we thank you, dear Lord, for judging us not justly but mercifully; for dealing with us not on the basis of our goodness but yours; and for coming to us not because you need us but because we need you. We praise your name for not forsaking us in our low estate, for stooping to us in our depths that you might lift us to your heights.

Yet our gratitude mingles with guilt. We bow in shame before the treachery of our ancestors. Then we pause to examine ourselves, and we are more ashamed than ever. For even with their mistakes plainly before us, we repeat them as if they had never been made. Even with their confessions clearly before us, we shelve them as if they had never been uttered. But in the end we learn, as they learned, that from your presence there is no hiding place; and that the hound of heaven will never stop running after us until we stop running from ourselves.

For this folly, O God, we beg your forgiveness. The breach between you and us is wide, but it is of *our* making and not yours. We are the transgressors, but we are not proud of our transgressions. We are especially sorry for duplicating the mistakes of our ancestors. Enable us now, O God, to put the sinful past behind us, theirs and ours, that we might embrace the hopeful future with confidence.

Raise our vision beyond our daily routine to the distant horizons of your sovereign rule. Let us no longer walk through the world as self-centered dreamers. Grant us the sensitivity of our Lord that we too might be moved from complacency to action. And let our action, like his, be rendered with an eye only to your will for the human family and without regard for personal risk to ourselves.

As we consider the summons of Jesus to deny ourselves, take up the cross and follow him, let us remember this simple truth: for us as for him, crossbearing is a way of living before becoming a way of dying.

Benediction. The journey of Jesus took him into a world of suffering, rejection, and death. As we go into this same world, embolden us, O God, that we too might take up our cross and follow you. Teach us to ask not that you shield us from temptation, but that you keep us from evil in temptation's midst.

Third Sunday in Lent

Lections: Exodus 20:1-17; Psalm 19; I Corinthians 1:18-25; John 2:13-22

Call to Worship
L: The foolishness of God is wiser than human wisdom.
P: Disclose to us your foolishness, Lord, that we might become wise.
L: The weakness of God is stronger than human strength.
P: Reveal to us your weakness, Lord, that we might become strong.

A: Let us worship the Lord who, on Calvary, turned foolishness into wisdom, weakness into strength, and a cross of torture into a tree of life.

Invocation. O God, the light of our life and the hope of our world, we come before you with clouded minds and restless hearts. We cannot make peace with ourselves until we make peace with you. So we pray that you will let the sun of your love burst upon us in all its glory. Let its raging fire burn away the shame of our sin. Let its healing warmth purify the motives of our hearts. And let its transforming light reveal the person in whose image you made us, that we might worship you as you are and serve you as we ought.

Litany
L: The Lord delivers us from bondage that we might become the people of God.
P: We shall have no god before us but the Lord.
L: The Lord delivers us from bondage that we might become the people of God.
P: We shall worship no image in the Lord's name.
L: The Lord delivers us from bondage that we might become the people of God.
P: We shall celebrate the Sabbath in the Lord's name.
L: The Lord delivers us from bondage that we might become the people of God.
P: We shall honor our parents in the Lord's name.
L: The Lord delivers us from bondage that we might become the people of God.
P: We shall serve our neighbors in the Lord's name.
A: Let the words of our mouths, the meditations of our hearts, and the deeds of our hands be acceptable in your sight, O Lord, our Strength and our Redeemer.

Prayer for One Voice. O God, who has endowed us with a thirst that you alone can quench, a hunger that you alone can satisfy, and a restlessness that you alone can still, we turn to you in adoration and prayer. We turn to you because there is no one else to whom we can turn, confident of finding answers to our questions and quiet for our souls. In vain we have looked elsewhere for succor. So now we seek you, counting on your promise that mourners shall be comforted, the weak strengthened, the foolish made wise, and crossbearers vindicated. We thank you, O God, not only for inviting us to call upon you in our hour of need, but for receiving us not as beggars but as friends.

We do not deserve such a welcome. Our words and thoughts and deeds have raised a wall of hostility against you. You gave the law as a lamp unto our feet, but we have cast it into a weapon for attacking others. You delivered the Commandments as signposts for the way, but we have treated them as statutes for passing judgment. You entrusted us with the testimonies of your unmerited love, but we have twisted them into proofs of our superior virtue. You gave us the light that we might help others find the path of discipleship, but by refusing that light we have helped obscure it. By spurning your offer of communion, we have closed the channels of grace for others.

So we implore your forgiveness, O God, not only for our unwitting detours off the path of love but for all those whom we have led astray. Let us rediscover the transforming power of a faithful relationship with you; so that, instead of conscripting you into the service of our religion, we shall enlist our religion in your service.

As we reflect on our Lord's impatience with the money-changers who turned the house of God into a house of trade, we cannot help sympathizing with the victims of his wrath. We too have been tempted to mistake the adornment of our sanctuary for the fulfillment of our mission. So we humbly pray, O God, that you will save us:

From assuming that a gift for the church is a gift for God;

From talking more about what people do for the church than about what the church does for people;

From taking greater pride in bringing the world into the church than in sending the church into the world;

From elevating the servants of your Word into rulers of our congregations;

From forgetting that we must sometimes oppose the prescriptions of religion for the sake of truth.

Help us this day, O Lord, to rediscover the church as the Body of Christ and ourselves as its members, each caring for the others and all working for you. Continue the work through this, your second body, that you began in Nazareth of Galilee.

Benediction. Go forth among your neighbors as ambassadors of the Lord, your eyes enlightened with God's commandments, your minds quickened with God's testimonies, your hearts rejoicing in God's law, and your souls aflame with God's love.

Fourth Sunday in Lent

Lections: Numbers 21:4-9; Psalm 107:1-3, 17-22; Ephesians 2:1-10; John 3:14-21

Call to Worship
L: In sadness we remember the days of our exile;
P: We called upon the Lord, and the Lord heard our cry.
L: In gladness we celebrate our deliverance from bondage;
P: The Lord heeded our summons, and the Lord brought us home.
A: O come, let our praise of the Lord resound! O come, let us sing the songs of Zion!

Invocation. Almighty and gracious God, who does not trade love for love but gives love without price, who does not return evil for evil but renders good for evil, who does not crucify sinners but dies in their place, we are as helpless to explain your ways as we are anxious to share your presence. So we make bold to ask for the gift of your presence in our congregation and for the guidance of your Spirit in our worship.

Litany
L: How can we sing the Lord's song? We live in a land whose culture puts ease before ethics.
P: Jesus lived in such a land, yet *he* sang the Lord's song.
L: How can we sing the Lord's song? We live in a land whose business puts success before service.

P: Jesus lived in such a land, yet he sang the Lord's song.

L: How can we sing the Lord's song? We live in a land whose politics puts power before principle.

P: Jesus lived in such a land, yet he sang the Lord's song.

L: How can we sing the Lord's song? We live in a land whose religion puts conformity before conscience.

P: Jesus lived in such a land, yet he sang the Lord's song.

L: How can we sing the Lord's song? The faithful life is a lonely life.

A: Jesus has promised that, as the Lord was in him, so shall the Lord be in us.

Prayer for One Voice. O God, who in nature displays matchless power and who in Christ manifests marvelous grace, we bow before you in grateful adoration. We are moved to awe by your power; we are moved to shame by your grace. We rejoice in your goodness and your greatness. For if your goodness were as ours, you would not redeem us; and if your greatness were as ours, you *could* not redeem us. We thank you, O Lord of heaven and earth, that your goodness is equal to our need; that your greatness is a match for your goodness; that you can and do redeem us.

Like the Israelites in Babylon, we know what it is to live in a foreign land. But unlike the Israelites, *our* exile was not inflicted by others. We became exiles by choice. Even though we were made for you, we strayed from your path like lost sheep. Some of us joined the prodigal in the far country. And when our captors tormented us, saying, "Sing us the songs of Zion," we complied. We sang the songs of Zion to the tunes of life in the fast lane. Big bucks, easy virtue, selfish indulgence: these became our gods and defined our goals. But others of us, like the elder brother, became exiles from your presence at home. We did not travel to the far country, yet we became as estranged from you as if we had. We remembered Jerusalem, but only to rebuke it for not delivering the privileges we were promised. We still sang the songs of Zion to the old tunes, but we did it from habit and not from the heart. The church was never open when we were not there; the offerings were never taken that we did not contribute; helpers were never sought that we did not volunteer. We lamented the disregard of our studied piety: "Why," we asked, "are we not given the credit due us? And why, when the prodigals return home, is such a fuss made over them?"

No matter the class of prodigals to which we belong—whether the vagabond or the home-grown—we are homesick for your presence, O God. We are weighed down in bondage to the sin that sent us into exile, and we long to be free again. Pardon our iniquity, O Lord. Unfurl your mighty arm, deliver us with your victorious right hand, set our feet upon your path, and we shall walk in your way, heed your word, and obey your law.

As we return home to you, O Lord, we are mindful of the multitudes who grope in the day as in the night. They, too, are exiles—perhaps not from you, but from freedom and dignity—and they hunger and thirst after equality and justice. They, too, long for deliverance. Make us conscious not only of your desire to satisfy that longing, but of our responsibility for its fulfillment. If they bear their suffering alone, make us aware of our guilt. If we greet their protest in silence, convict us of our cowardice. If we tolerate the boast of their oppressors, shatter our assumption of innocence. Empower us to be faithful to you, O Lord, and we shall be faithful to them.

Let the love that lifted Jesus' first disciples lift us. Raise our vision to the mountaintops, enabling us to scale the heights and leave behind the land and life of our exile forever.

Benediction. As the Lord sent Jesus into the world to manifest the grace of God, the Lord sends us into the world to manifest the love of Christ. Go now in the assurance that, as the Lord stood with Jesus in the hour of his trial, the Lord shall stand with us in the hour of our trial. As the Lord went with him, the Lord shall go with us.

Fifth Sunday in Lent

Lections: Jeremiah 31:31-34; Psalm 51:1-12; Hebrews 5:5-10; John 12:20-33

Call to Worship
L: The hour comes, and now is, says the Lord, when I will make a new covenant with my people.

P: It shall not be written upon tablets of stone, but upon the tablets of the heart.

L: We shall no longer instruct our neighbors from a book.

P: They shall no longer need any teacher but the Lord.

A: Waken our ears, O Lord, and speak to us the words of your covenant.

Invocation. O God, with whom we have set ourselves at odds and from whom we have gone astray, the separation between us would have been final but for you. The more we tried to break free from you, the harder you sought to keep hold of us. And finally, O Lord, you brought us back, not with a yoke of iron, but with a yoke of love. Now that we are home in your tender embrace, let us freely take upon ourselves your yoke, for your yoke is easy, and your burden is light.

Litany

L: In Jesus Christ, God replaced the old covenant with the new, the law written on stone with that written on the heart, our separation *from* God with our reconciliation *to* God.

P: Let us, therefore, seek God's grace, that we might leave behind the chaff of separation and bring forth the harvest of reconciliation.

L: We are not content merely to deny the existence of other gods.

P: We affirm the exclusive claim on our lives by the Lord.

L: We are not content merely to cease using the Lord's name in vain.

P: We lift the name of the Lord our God in wonder and in praise.

L: We are not content merely to avoid taking our neighbors' life.

P: We bless them as we would have them bless us.

L: We are not content merely to refrain from stealing their possessions.

P: We strive earnestly to discover and meet their needs.

L: We are not content merely to keep from coveting their good fortune.

71

P: We go out of our way to assure that good fortune comes their way.

L: Now, therefore, if we will obey the law of the covenant written on our hearts, we shall be the Lord's people forever.

P: All that the Lord has written we will do, and we will be obedient.[20]

Prayer for One Voice. O Lord, by whose grace slaves were set free and no people became your people, we too have felt your slave-liberating, people-making power. We worship you not only for the gracious past our ancestors shaped for us; we worship you also for the glorious future we are shaping for our descendants. We come unto you because you first came unto us; we seek you because you first sought us; and we love you because you first loved us. We are not your people because we chose you to be our God. We are your people because you chose us to be your people, and for this we give thanks.

But like the covenant-breakers of old, we have confused the roles of the Chooser and the chosen. You gave us a pen to write your law upon our hearts, but *our* voice guided the hand as it wrote. The law we inscribed there was all too often not yours but ours. You intended it as an instrument of liberation, but we have fashioned it into a tool of legalism. We no longer lay our animals on the altar of sacrifice, but neither do we lay ourselves on the altar of service. We no longer offend you with our presentation of burnt offerings, but neither do we please you with our presentation of contrite hearts. Forgive us, O God, for our mindless repetition of the folly of our ancestors, and renew with us the promise you made to them, for the sake of *our* descendants. Forgive our iniquity, and remember our sin no more, that we may know you as you know us and love our neighbors as you love them. Create in us a new heart, that we might break the old habits that estranged us. Deliver us from attachment to the land of our exile, that we might never again feel at home except in your presence.

We study the Gospel lesson with a mixture of joy and guilt.

---

[20] See Exodus 19:5; 24:7.

We are delighted that sometimes strangers still come to us, saying, "We would know Jesus." At the same time, we reproach ourselves that it happens so rarely. In ways unknown to us and in ways too well known to us, we have hidden him from view. We have contradicted our witness, invalidated our testimony, and betrayed our mission.

We pray, O Lord, for ourselves as individuals and for the church as a people, that your spirit will descend upon us and remake us from the inside out. Lift the scales from our eyes so that, when we look upon a world inhabited by diverse races and cultures, we shall behold the members of your family and ours. Render our hearts of stone into hearts of flesh so that, when we look at pictures of starving children, we shall behold the objects of your compassion and ours. And heal the paralysis of our limbs so that, when we look at the victims of injustice, we shall behold the beneficiaries of your redemption and ours. Christ has been lifted up; let him draw all people unto you, O God. So incline our hearts unto you that we shall hasten this global reunion of your people.

Benediction. O God, you send us forth not into the world in which Jesus was born but into the world in which we were born. You will not save us *from* our world, because you have saved us *for* our world. And you have promised to go with us into that world, enabling us to do even greater works than those of Jesus. Go with us, dear Lord, and we shall become the keepers of your promise.

Passion/Palm Sunday

Lections: Isaiah 50:4-9*a;* Psalm 118:19-29; Philippians 2:5-11; Mark 14-15

Call to Worship
L: O come, let us worship the One whom God has highly exalted—
P: Who, though being in the form of God, did not count deity a title to claim.

L: O come, let us worship the One whom God has highly exalted—

P: Who, though being in the form of God, did not count humanity a form to despise.

L: O come, let us worship the one whom God has highly exalted—

A: Let us worship the Lord in the name of Jesus and confess our faith in God.

Invocation. O Lord, whose victory in Jerusalem culminated in agony on Golgotha, deliver us from the temptation to turn your very real passion into a pious parade. Remind us that your destination on that first Palm Sunday was not a festive coronation in the Holy City but a final confirmation from God; that you spurned the offer of a royal crown to shoulder the shame of a criminal's cross; that you were able to save others only because you did not seek to save yourself; and that, for us as for you, the cost of divine approval demands the devotion of our will to God's.

Litany

L: This is the day to remember Jesus' journey from Jerusalem to Calvary:

P: The day to remember the deeds of those who inflicted the pain;

L: The day to remember the acts of those who partook of the burdens;

P: The day to remember that we, like the chief priests, betray the Lord by stealth;

L: The day to remember that we, like the woman with the ointment, owe the Lord our best;

P: The day to remember that we, like Judas, sell the Lord for silver;

L: The day to remember that we, like Pilate, reject conscience for the crowd;

P: The day to remember that we, like Simon of Cyrene, can bear the Savior's cross;

A: The day to remember that we, like Jesus, must die to self to live for God.

Prayer for One Voice. O God, who in Jesus became a member of our family that we might become members of your family, your grace astounds and confounds us. We stand amazed at the cost of our redemption. You turned away from no one, yet all turned away from you. You came to the members of your own household, but they greeted you as a stranger. You came to the members of your own synagogue, but they treated you as an alien. You came to the leaders of your own religion, but they dismissed you as a blasphemer. You came to the inner circle of your own disciples, but they forsook you as a loser. You came before the governor, and he offered you as a scapegoat.

Many of us have been tested, but our response has not been the same. Watching you, we can only echo the exclamation of the centurion, "Truly you are the Son of God." So today, like your disciples on that first Palm Sunday, we spread our branches and garments before you. In this way we glorify you, O Christ, not merely for the fact of your revelation of God, but for the manner of that revelation. By demonstrating the possibility of our union with God, you imply that we are responsible for our separation from God. Nevertheless, we are encouraged. Not only are we heartened by the assurance that our dreams and our deeds can become one. We are also reassured that the power of God will make them one.

As we relate the story of Jesus' entry into Jerusalem, we are confronted by the revelation not only of you but of us. We see you in the actions of Christ; ourselves, in the actions of those who turned his triumph into tragedy. The maneuvering of the chief priests and scribes, the avarice of Judas, the noisy boast of Peter, the drowsiness of the inner circle, the cry of the rabble, the mockery of the soldiers, the taunts of the passersby: this catalogue of sins is all but endless and all too familiar. We have experienced many of them, firsthand.

Lord, we may not have been there when they crucified you then, but we are here when they crucify you now. Forgive us for siding with the crucifiers against the Crucified. And restore to us the joy of our salvation, that we may carry the cross with as much fervor as we sing about it.

There are many people for whom we should intercede, but

we especially single out the victims of our faithless witness: those who look to us for generosity, but are repelled by our greed; those who look to us for boldness, but are put off by our hesitation; those who look to us for forthrightness, but are muted by our silence; those who look to us for compassion, but are stunned by our indifference; those who look to us for constancy, but are startled by our fickleness.

Deliver us, O Lord, from the weakness with which we have victimized those who have turned to us for strength. And fill us with your spirit, so that, when we stumble, they will not fall. Help them stand because they follow not our example but yours—the example of the one who set his face steadfastly toward Jerusalem,[21] even though he knew it would bring rejection and suffering.

Benediction. O Lord, send us back into our workaday world, chastened by the knowledge that we too are capable of the treachery to which even your closest friends succumbed; comforted by the assurance that, just as you did not forsake them, you will not forsake us; and strengthened by the certainty that you can change us, as them, from fickle friends into faithful disciples.

Holy Thursday

Lections: Exodus 12:1-14; Psalm 116:1-2, 12-19; I Corinthians 11:23-26; John 13:1-17, 31b-35

Call to Worship
L: We gather to commemorate our Lord's observance of the Jewish Passover,
P: Which ends with the people's pledge, "All that the Lord has spoken we will do, and we will be faithful."
L: We gather to commemorate our Lord's institution of Holy Communion,
P: Which ends with the Lord's assurance, "This is my blood of the covenant, which is poured out for many."

---

[21] See Luke 9:51.

L: We gather to celebrate Holy Communion and renew our covenant with the Lord and one another.

A: All that the Lord shall speak we will do, and we will be faithful.

Invocation. O Merciful God, tonight we take our place at table with our Lord. When he predicts our betrayal, let us examine not our neighbors but ourselves. When he predicts our falling away, let us remember that the crow of the cock is more predictable than any of us. As we contemplate his imminent arrest, let us feel not only the pain of our great loss but the shame of our tragic guilt. Then, as we anticipate his impending death, empower us so to live that he shall not have died in vain.

Litany

L: Jesus was the victim of circumstances beyond his control.

P: Therefore, he can understand us when we are forced to risk long odds.

L: Yet his helplessness before people never altered his trust in the Lord.

P: Therefore, he can deliver us when we are tempted to abandon the struggle.

L: In our hour of trial, when we are beset by an enemy,

P: Help us to remember you, O Lord, in your hour of trial.

L: When we are betrayed for personal gain,

P: Help us to remember you, O Lord.

L: When we are left to face a crisis alone,

P: Help us to remember you, O Lord.

L: When we see a stranger where we had expected a friend,

P: Help us to remember you, O Lord, in your hour of trial.

L: In our hour of trial, when others have done to us their worst,

P: Help us to remember you, O Lord, in your hour of trial, and how that nothing in life or death was able to separate you from the love of God.[22]

---

[22] See Romans 8:38 f.

Prayer for One Voice. Holy Thursday reminds us of the power and the peril of friendship. Despite the beauty of Jesus' love for the Twelve, there came the tragedy of their betrayal. Yet, even after his disciples had forsaken him, he was not alone. You were there—as comforter, friend, and guide—to hear his cry of distress, to assure him of your presence, and to receive his spirit.

We adore you, dear Lord, for standing by him in his hour of trial and for standing by us in ours. No matter how fierce our foes or how fickle our friends, you are with us. So we thank you, dear Lord, for *your* friendship—a friendship that, even at our best, we could never deserve, and that, even at our worst, we could never destroy.

We wish, O Lord, that we could say that we have learned from the mistakes of the first disciples. But, as we review the crimes committed by the Twelve against Jesus, we are pressed to name a single one for which we could not also be indicted. They failed to make promises that they should have made, and they failed to keep some of the promises that they did make. Let us rebuke them if we dare, but let us not forget *our* promises, unmade and unkept. The Twelve, despite personal instruction by Jesus, never really understood him: despite his warning that his mission was certain to attract enemies, they fled once those enemies showed their hand; after pledging to follow him to the death, they denied having known him and left him, friendless, before his accusers. Let us rebuke them if we dare, but let us not forget *our* transgressions, witting and unwitting.

It is not the Twelve or the Seventy or even our brothers and our sisters who stand most in need of prayer. It is we—we who have misunderstood and betrayed and deserted you, we who have left you alone to face your enemies and ours. Wherefore, dear Lord, we ask not only for your forgiveness, but for the renewal of your spirit in us.

As we partake together of the one cup and the one loaf, let us be reminded that they attest to our unity—our unity with friends like ourselves, weak, rebellious, and fickle; and our unity with you, O Lord, the friend who counters weakness with strength, rebellion with obedience, and fickleness with faithfulness. Let our communion be more than a participation in your death. Let it also be an extension of your life.

Benediction. O Lord, when we came into your house, we promised to offer you the sacrifice of thanksgiving. Now, as we leave your house, we promise to obey all your commandments. Help us be as diligent in keeping our vow of obedience as we were in keeping our vow of thanksgiving.

Good Friday

Lections: Isaiah 52:13–53:12; Psalm 22; Hebrews 4:14-16; 5:7-9; John 18–19

Call to Worship
L: We do not gather to worship a Christ unfamiliar with our limitations.
P: We come to worship the Christ who took our limitations unto himself.
L: We do not gather to worship a Christ who lays *his* cross upon us.
P: We come to worship the Christ who takes *our* cross upon himself.
A: O come, let us worship the Christ who reveals the divinity of true humanity!

Invocation. O Christ, help us relive this day in your life that we may relive your life in our day. You went to your death—the innocent for the guilty, the gentle for the violent, the obedient for the rebellious—opening not your mouth. Now we have learned that, before our world can experience a resurrection like yours, we must experience a death like yours. Teach us how to die as you died, O Christ, that we might live as you lived—for God, enduring the cross and despising the shame.

Litany
L: On this, a most faithful and a most fateful day in the long history of God's people, we reach the climax in the unfolding drama of the life and ministry of Jesus.

P: We confess, O Lord, that this is a fateful day because we have been a faithless people.

L: We have been too much like the innkeeper, who could not find room in his inn for Jesus; and the rich young ruler, who could not find room in his life for Jesus; and even Herod, who could not find room in his world for Jesus.

P: We confess, O Lord, that this is a fateful day because we have been a faithless people.

L: We have been too much like James and John, who promised to follow you, but demanded the choice seats in your kingdom; and Peter, who hailed you as the Christ, but denied knowing the suffering servant; and even Judas, who loved you much, but betrayed you for thirty pieces of silver.

P: We confess, O Lord, that this is a fateful day because we have been a faithless people.

L: We have been too much like the Pilate who wanted to release Jesus, but released Barabbas; and the Pilate who could find no fault in Jesus, but left him to the mercy of those who did; and even the Pilate who could have prevented the crucifixion, but chose instead to wash his hands.

P: We confess, O Lord, that this is a fateful day because we have been a faithless people.

L: As we recall the cross you chose to bear in taking our side, we remember the crosses we have shunned to avoid taking your side.

A: O Christ, who was faithful to God unto death, grant us the grace to be faithful unto you in life.

Prayer for One Voice. O God, in Jesus you became subject to us that we might become subject to you. Your reconciling presence was at work in his ministry, and not merely when he was in control, healing and teaching and preaching. It was no less at work in him when others were in control, betraying, mocking and crucifying him. This we firmly believe. We are witnesses to the gospel that you were in Jesus reconciling the world, not only after the resurrection and Pentecost, but in his rejection and suffering and death.

We thank you, O God, for revealing in him the mind you intend for us all, proclaiming through your incarnation in him the possibility of your incarnation in us. It is no more blasphemous to say we can be like him than to say he was like you. He was the Son of man *and* the Son of God; Jesus of earth and Christ of heaven. And he was the prophet who declared, "You shall do greater works than these."[23]

Yet we have been slow to follow the example of our Servant Lord in suffering for the sins of others. Worse yet, we have denied responsibility for our own sins. And we have excused ourselves by blaming our troubled times. We should have thought, instead, of the troubled times of Jesus, and how that he, when friends forsook him, appealed his case to a higher court; how that he, when even that appeal brought no justice, was faithful unto death; and how that he, in death as in life, showed the way to you.

O God, when our neighbors come to us in search of direction, help us point them beyond their weakness to your greatness, that you might do for them through us what you have done for us through others.

Benediction. O Christ, as you answered God's call to live for others, you have called us to go and do likewise. Occasionally we have, but living for others has yet to become our way of life. So we pray, dear Lord, for the vision to find this way and the courage to take it.

---

[23] See John 14:12.

Easter Season

Easter

Lections: Acts 10:34-43; Psalm 118:14-24; I Corinthians 15:1-11; John 20:1-18

Call to Worship
L: From a world that leaves the just to the mercy of the strong,
P: We come to worship the God who turns crosses into crowns.
L: With hearts that long for the victory of life but fear the triumph of death,
P: We come to worship the God who turns the vanquished into victors.
A: Thanks be to God, who gives us the victory through our Lord Jesus Christ.[24]

Invocation. Almighty God, on Calvary you chose the foolish to shame the wise, the weak to defy the strong, and the despised to mock the proud. Today we gather together not merely to applaud your choice but to ask for its repetition in us. Deliver us from the self-righteous addiction of the cruci-fiers that we might know the self-giving affection of the Crucified. Grant us the power to proclaim the Easter promise of participation in the conquest of Christ by living out the commitment of Jesus.

Litany
L: O God of Jesus Christ, who welcomed the company of the lowly in his labor for the holy,
P: Grant us his spirit, who came into the world not to be served but to serve.

---

[24] See I Corinthians 15:57.

L: O God of Jesus Christ, who rebuked the praise of the pious in his demand for justice,

P: Grant us his spirit, who proclaimed the gospel not only in word but in deed.

L: O God of Jesus Christ, who braved the wrath of the mighty in his fidelity to the Almighty,

P: Grant us his spirit, who was obedient not only in death but also in life.

L: O God of Jesus Christ, who forgave the taunts of the scorners in his agony on Calvary,

P: Grant us his spirit, who kindled belief not only in his disciples but also in his enemies.

L: O God of Jesus Christ, who transformed the despair of his followers by his victory on Easter,

A: Grant us his spirit, who was triumphant not only over death but also over sin.

Prayer for One Voice. Almighty God, who set the sun in the heavens to light up the earth by day and the moon and the stars by night, you sent Jesus Christ to earth to light up our life by day and by night. We celebrate your gift of life. As you chased the shadows of the deep, you have shattered the darkness of Calvary. Now we know that nothing can ever again separate us from the light with which you flood all creation in Jesus Christ.

O light of the world, on Easter you dug the grave of darkness. Today we commemorate your victory, not only of light over darkness and life over death, but of love over hate and meaning over mystery. We thank you for Easter's reversal of Good Friday. We had heard of your judgments by the mouths of the prophets, but now we have confirmation of them from the Lord of life: that you judge not by what the eyes see and the ears hear but by what justice requires and truth demands; that you judge not with favor for the mighty but with equity for the meek; that you decide not with rewards for oppressors but with amends for the oppressed.

Yet our acts of pride compromise our words of praise. We more often echo the prophets' pronouncements of divine judgment with our lips than with our lives. Our love does not render us blind to the sights or deaf to the sounds of selfish ambition. Our love does not check our preference for the company of the mighty over the meek. Our love does not move us to champion the cause of the oppressed against oppressors. We call ourselves your Easter people, but we daily resurrect the life that Jesus crucified.

We are not what you would have us be. Yet we long to become what you would have us become. So we pray, O Lord, not only for the forgiveness of our deafness and blindness and silence, but we pray also for your renewal of our hearing and sight and speech. Open our ears to the cries of the deprived and the depraved, lest our deafness continue to aggravate the misery of the miserable. Open our eyes to the plight of the sick and hungry, lest our blindness compound the neglect of the neglected. Loose our tongues to proclaim the promise of life, lest Easter be reduced to a memory of the past without meaning for the present.

O risen Christ, who joined a company of your disciples on the Emmaus Road, we are grateful that your walk among us did not end in Emmaus; that, even now, you go before us to show us the way to your mission and ours. We can do all things through you who strengthens us. You break down the middle wall of partition, that you might reconcile us to God in one body. Empower us, dear Lord, to become faithful witnesses to your wall-breaking gospel of reconciliation. Do it, we beseech you, not in spite of us but through us. Make us one in our witness to the triumph of Easter, that we might become one in our witness to the God of Easter.

O Light of the world, illumine our hearts, that we might feel your compassion; illumine our minds, that we might discern your will; and illumine our path, that we might carry your mission to the ends of the earth, through Jesus Christ our Lord.

Benediction. O God, who in Jesus Christ turned the defeat of Good Friday into the victory of Easter, bringing dawn out of darkness and life out of death, make us faithful witnesses to the life-giving power of your crossbearing love. Keep us ever mindful of the Risen One's promise that we would do even greater works than he. And send us forth, with hope renewed and zeal aflame, to labor in the vineyard of the Lord.

Second Sunday of Easter

Lections: Acts 4:32-35; Psalm 133; I John 1:1–2:2; John 20:19-31

Call to Worship
L: Let us praise God for the mighty deeds wrought through Jesus Christ.
P: Praise God for loosing the chains of sin!
L: Let us praise God for the mighty deeds wrought through Jesus Christ.
P: Praise God for breaking the bonds of death!
L: Let us praise God for the mighty deeds wrought through Jesus Christ.
P: Praise God for releasing the forces of love!
A: Let us join with God's people everywhere and praise Jesus Christ the Lord!

Invocation. O Christ, whose birth means nothing unless we be born of love, whose life means nothing unless we live for God, whose death means nothing unless we die unto self, and whose resurrection means nothing unless we rise unto newness of life, we praise your holy name. Let our lips utter no desire that does not proceed from a committed heart. And let our mouths express no thought that does not spring from a faithful spirit.

Litany
L: The company of believers is of one heart and mind.
P: With great power they witness to the resurrection of Jesus.
L: They do not hoard possessions, but distribute to each according to need.
P: With great power they witness to the resurrection of Jesus.
L: They do not clamor for recognition, but outdo one another in showing honor.

85

P: With great power they witness to the resurrection of Jesus.

L: They do not stand in awe of the rich, but they go the second mile for the lowly.

P: With great power they witness to the resurrection of Jesus.

L: They pay the earthly powers their dues, but they obey God rather than rulers.

P: With great power they witness to the resurrection of Jesus.

L: They are too strong to abuse their freedom, yet they are too mindful of the weak to indulge their strength.

A: How good and pleasant it is when disciples, like Christ, please not self but God.

Prayer for One Voice. O God, who in Jesus sent your life to earth and on Easter revealed your power over death, we bless you in the name of Christ our Lord. We cannot know the risen Christ as Thomas demanded to know him. We cannot touch the print of the nails in his hands or gaze at the wounds in his side. But we can know him in the power of his resurrection. Jesus left us, but he did not leave us alone. Before taking his leave of earth, he breathed your spirit on his disciples, enabling them to recall his words and deeds and to interpret them.

That same spirit is still at work. Not only does it enable Christ to become our contemporary; it enables us to become contemporary with Christ. We do not have to envy those first disciples. For just as Christ became their companion on the Emmaus Road, he becomes our companion on the roads we travel. As he walked with them, he walks with us. And if we will but listen, he will also talk with us. Moreover, if we will walk in his steps, he will claim us as his own.

O Lord of heaven and earth, who was never more truly present with us than when you joined humankind in Christ, we adore you for revealing yourself in Jesus, as you were and are and evermore shall be. As we thank you for him, we thank you also for those who have kept his spirit alive. Their name may not be Legion, but their presence is undeniable.

As he gave himself to your mission, they give themselves to his mission. As he bore witness to the unity between God and humankind, they bear witness to the unity between Christ and the church.

Yet our life as a Christian community has rarely moved outsiders to exclaim that we are one with Jesus. Unlike those who did evoke this testimony, we are not of one mind and one spirit. We betray our claim to unity with you by our practice of divisions among ourselves.

Forgive us, dear Lord, for this betrayal of those who come to us in search of bread for the journey. We cannot but feel guilty that our love has not been more generous: that oppressors have looked to us for silence, and not in vain; that the victims of the system have looked to us for justice, but in vain.

As we intercede in prayer for these victims of our faithlessness, send us forth to put life into our words. Restore their faith in you through our demonstration of faith in them. Awaken us to your will, that we may awaken them to your will. Renew your partnership with us so that your spirit will infuse our partnership with them. And let us and them, hand in hand with you and one another, go into the world to perform the mission to which Christ has commissioned us. Let us not forget that, in faith as in life, we all rely on mentors. Grant us the grace, dear Lord, so to represent you that we will neither displease you nor mislead others.

Benediction. O God, as you have brought us together to think the thoughts of Christ, send us forth to do the deeds of Christ. Let the affections of our hearts and the deeds of our hands proclaim our devotion to you and our love for one another.

Third Sunday of Easter

Lections: Acts 3:12-19; Psalm 4; I John 3:1-7; Luke 24:36*b*-48

Call to Worship
L: Come, let us worship and bow down; let us kneel before Christ, our Redeemer—

P: Who was anointed by the spirit of God to bring good news to the poor.

L: Come, let us worship and bow down; let us kneel before Christ, our Redeemer—

P: Who was crucified by the keepers of order for heeding the summons of God.

L: Come, let us worship and bow down; let us kneel before Christ, our Redeemer—

P: Who baptizes us with the Holy Spirit for bringing the reign of God to earth.

A: Come, let us worship and bow down; let us kneel before Christ, our Redeemer!

Invocation. O God, who chased the gloom of the disciples with the gospel of Easter and drowned their desert of despair in a sea of grace, surprise us this day. Take from us the presumption that leans on our strength instead of yours, that mistakes our wisdom for yours, and equates our will with yours. Assure us once again that our Lord's promise to be with us always still holds good. And be present with us now, as in the days of Jesus, to make us whole and to make us holy.

Litany

L: O God, who through your power at work in Jesus made the old feel young and the young feel mature, we pray for the outpouring of your power upon our generation.

P: Baptize our generation in the spirit with which Jesus baptized his.

L: Instead of lamenting our inability to work miracles of healing, make us supporters of the medicine that can make the lame walk, the deaf hear, and the blind see.

P: Baptize our generation!

L: Instead of lamenting our inability to turn children into geniuses, make us backers of the education that can inspire the gifted to care, the average to think, and the slow to try.

P: Baptize our generation!

L: Instead of lamenting our inability overnight to rid the world of poverty, make us shapers of the programs that will provide food for the hungry, shelter for the homeless, and clothing for the deprived.

P: Baptize our generation!

L: Instead of lamenting our inability to tame hardened criminals, make us designers of plans that can turn anger into resolve, despair into hope, and aimlessness into ambition.

P: Baptize our generation!

L: Instead of lamenting our inability to make our neighbors take notice of us, make us doers of deeds that will turn their attention to you.

A: Baptize our generation in the spirit with which Jesus baptized his. Pour out your power upon us!

Prayer for One Voice. O God, who in Jesus revealed the love that endows life with significance, the purpose that gives direction to humanity, and the power that spells death for evil, you are our Lord and a great God above all gods. We worship you, for your revelation in Jesus will not permit us to offer you anything less than our worship.

For this manifestation of your grace, we thank you, dear Lord. From this storehouse of riches we have continually drawn, yet the treasury has not been depleted. For like all the spiritual capital with which you have entrusted us, it is something we can lose only by failing to use it. This truth you have written deep into the heart of us all. We thank you, gracious Lord, for thus ordering our existence. Not only does it mean that we can find purpose for our life. It also demands that we respect the lives of others.

Yet we cannot ponder your gift without asking forgiveness for its abuse. We may be quick to hail the power of Jesus' name, but we are slow to spread our trophies at his feet: we are as apt to expect him to crown us as we are to crown him. He has opened our minds that we may understand the Scriptures, but we have hardened our hearts against his interpretation of them. He has enacted the role of the Lord's suffering servant, but our faith becomes skeptical when "bad" things happen to "good" people. We sing that there is a cross for everyone, but we wait for Jesus to carry not only his but ours.

Paul proclaimed "Christ and him crucified," but we proclaim a gospel of ecstasy without agony. Whereas for Jesus Calvary was a way of life, we have turned it into a way of death. And whereas Easter marked your stamp of approval on Jesus' way of life, we have reduced the resurrection to a proof of the immortality of the soul. Forgive us, O God, for thus mocking the meaning and message of our Lord Jesus Christ.

We pray, O Lord, that you will so rule our hearts that we will make you known not only in the breaking of the bread but in the sharing of the bread: that we shall shoulder the cross you carried for the poor and oppressed; that we shall recognize that repentance, like charity, must begin at home; that we shall accept the forgiveness of Christ, not merely as a revelation of the divine character, but as a model for human behavior; and that we shall bring into being the fellowship of kindred minds for which Jesus prayed.

O God, let us not lose sight of the connection between Easter and Good Friday. Let us remember that, if Easter demonstrates your ability to work the divine will without our help, Good Friday confirms that your victories do not come without cost to us. Deliver us from the lure of cheap grace. Make us as willing to pay the cost of your victories as we are to claim them for ourselves.

Benediction. O Lord, as you have made disciples of us, now you send us into the world to make disciples of others. Go with us and be our guide, that the witness of our lives may confirm the testimony of our lips.

Fourth Sunday of Easter

Lections: Acts 4:5-12; Psalm 23; I John 3:16-24; John 10:11-18

Call to Worship
L: O come, let us worship the Good Shepherd, for we are the sheep of his fold.

P: He gives us food from green pastures, he gives us water from pure fountains.

L: He plants our feet on safe paths, he leads us through dark valleys.

P: He protects us with his rod, he supports us with his staff.

L: He grants us asylum from our enemies, he offers us refuge with the righteous.

A: O come, let us worship the Good Shepherd, for we are the sheep of his fold.

Invocation. O God, when we claim wonders for you in the name of Jesus Christ, let us not forget that this stone—the head of the corner—is the same stone the builders rejected; that this Jesus—the manifestation of your glory—is the same Jesus who revealed the depths of human shame. Let us remember that we declare our faith, not by saying that Jesus was like you, but by saying that you are like Jesus. Set our minds on the glory of your presence, not in heaven or on earth, but in Jesus Christ our crucified Lord and Savior.

Litany

L: The Lord is our shepherd, but not ours alone, for the Lord has other sheep not of this fold.

P: So there shall be one flock and one shepherd.

L: The other folds include Baptists, Catholics, and Mennonites, but the Lord is their Shepherd, too.

P: So there shall be one flock and one shepherd.

L: The other folds include Muslims, Hindus, and Jews, but the Lord is their Shepherd, too.

P: So there shall be one flock and one shepherd.

L: The other folds include rightists, leftists, and centrists, but the Lord is their Shepherd, too.

P: So there shall be one flock and one shepherd.

L: The other folds include the learned, the ignorant, and the innocent, but the Lord is their Shepherd, too.

P: So there shall be one flock and one shepherd.

L: The other folds include peoples of every race under the sun, but the Lord is their Shepherd, too.

P: So there shall be one flock and one shepherd.

L: The other folds include peoples from every nation on earth, but the Lord is their Shepherd, too.

P: So there shall be one flock and one shepherd.

A: Help us, O Lord, to put the commands of our Shepherd before the claims of our fold.

Prayer for One Voice. O God, our Creator, when we consider humanity, we marvel at our endless variety. You have measured us with different yardsticks; some of us are small, others large. You have painted us with different brush strokes; we belong to diverse races. You have endowed us with different talents; some of us work with our hands, others with our minds. You have crowned us with glory and honor; you have put within our reach a marvelous harmony of sight and sound and sense. You have so made us that, apart from such harmony, we cannot experience the abundant life that you intend; that, if we would live the abundant life, we must acknowledge our dependence upon one another and upon you. To realize your purpose for us, we must so learn to care for one another that, when one of us suffers, we all suffer, and that, when one of us rejoices, we all rejoice.

Yet we have frustrated your purpose and turned your harmony into discord. We treasure the Scriptures that celebrate the quest for unity in diversity, yet we look with contempt on interpretations that depart from our own. We acknowledge you to be the Good Shepherd of the sheep of other folds, yet we foment conflict with the sheep of our own fold. Worse yet, we claim divine sanction for these divisions of our own making. And we proceed to justify our little love for one another by appeal to our devotion to Jesus Christ.

Forgive us, O God, not only for the ease with which we break communion with our brothers and sisters, but for the arrogance with which we lay the credit at your door. Save us from usurping your role as Judge, lest we be judged by the judgment with which we judge others.[25] Give us hearts that

---

25 See Matthew 7:2.

are generous as well as penitent: penitent, for we know how you deplore our pulling apart; and generous, for we know how you applaud our pulling together. We pray for the grace to strive for the unity of your fold. Bring us together in one flock, O God, that you may be the Good Shepherd of us all.

Benediction. O God, who takes no pleasure in creeds unmatched by deeds, let the works of our hands confirm the words of our lips. Curb our impulse to proclaim our faith apart from works, that by our works we may proclaim our faith.[26]

Fifth Sunday of Easter

Lections: Acts 8:26-40; Psalm 22:25-31; I John 4:7-21; John 15:1-8

Call to Worship
L: Come and sit with me; we shall study the Word.
P: Together we shall read and understand.
L: Come and kneel with me; we shall break the bread.
P: Together we shall eat and be satisfied.
L: Come and walk with me; we shall part the waters.
A: Together we shall risk, and, behold, we shall be changed.

Invocation. O Lord of the broken chain, the peoples of your earth seek their freedom. We kneel in the night, breathless runaways, breathing the silent prayer of the preyed upon.

O God of the North Star, we shall not be able to find our way unless someone guides us. Bend to us and lift our chins, and point our eyes to the brilliant light in the sky, that we may have a beacon upon which to fix our hopes. We have dared to stumble away from slave row, but unless you lead us, Lord, we can go no farther.

---

[26] See James 2:18.

LITANIES AND OTHER PRAYERS

Litany

L: The world arrested Christ our brother. It betrayed and bound him, it tested and mocked him, it tortured and killed him.

P: But he stood silent against the madness, and in that silence of his humiliation, justice was denied. It was betrayed and bound, it was tested and mocked, it was tortured and killed.

L: Who can describe the generation that took his life from the earth? Who can cleanse the hands that slaughtered the lamb?

P: O God, make of us another generation,

L: And let our hands be those not of murderers but midwives.

P: Let us not mock justice, but embrace it. Let us not take life, but deliver it.

L: Beloved, let us love one another; for love is of God, and whoever loves is born of God.

P: When our brothers are silenced by false accusers, let us be their voice. When our sisters appear before unjust judges, let us be their defender.

L: Let us bring our world to its knees before the Lord, that guilt may be declared.

P: And let us stand when God bids the world rise, that mercy may be granted.

L: For the Christ who was mortified at our hands has been glorified by the hand of God. His freedom has been restored and his life has been renewed,

A: That our world's captives might find their liberation and our world's dead, their resurrection.

Prayer for One Voice. O God, in the beginning you created heaven and earth. And, one day, as you walked upon the land, you came upon a very fertile hill and imagined there a vineyard purple with grapes. So with your own hands you dug it and cleared it of stones, and planted it with choice vines; long you tended it and looked for it to yield its fruit, but it yielded only wild grapes.[27]

---

[27] This and the following imagery is drawn from Isaiah 5.

94

No more could you have done for your vineyard, Lord. Your pleasant planting turned bitter and rebelled against you. You looked for justice, but, behold, we bore bloodshed; you looked for righteousness, but, behold, we produced a cry!

You could have become angry, Lord. You could have removed the hedge that protected the yard, that we might be devoured by the beasts. You could have broken down its wall, that we might be trampled. You could have laid it waste, and let our briers and thorns grow up; you could have commanded the clouds to withhold their rains, so that nothing would grow.

But even as you are our Creator and Sustainer, O God, you are our Redeemer. And you planted again in our midst. You set out at the center of the vineyard the true vine. And the vine has grown; it cannot be destroyed, it cannot bear bad fruit. Its good fruit hangs heavy on the branches, bearing witness to your care.

Christ is the vine, Lord; make us the branches. Whatever you ask us to be, we shall be; whatever you ask us to do, shall be done.

This truth amazes us, that you sent the true vine to save us not because we first loved you, but because you first and last loved us. By this we are humbled, Lord, for you are Alpha and Omega, Beginning and End, Love that began the beginning and knows no end. Yours is the love that birthed the world and makes it grow. It is the love that grasped Philip as he preached and drove him to carry the news of his new faith beyond the bounds of Judaism—even to places his old faith had considered unclean. It is the love that grasped the mighty Ethiopian as he sat in his chariot and drove him with a new faith into the waters of his baptism—to a new life his old life had never imagined.

Yours is the love, Lord, that changes the world, inside and out. The ones unclean in the world's eyes, your love makes clean. The ones mighty in the world's eyes, your love makes humble. The ones guilty in the world's eyes, your love ushers into paradise.

Lord, for this we praise you, that you first and last love us.

Now what remains is for you to teach us how better to love one another. Teach us, Lord, the truth of life, before the hour is late; lead us, Lord, in the way we should go, before the gate is closed.

Bring us now into your vineyard, Lord. Prune us and tend us, that we may bear good fruit. We offer you all that we are; press us into the wine of the new covenant, that the cup of the new kingdom may be filled to overflowing.

Benediction. No one has ever seen God. But, if an angel appears and tells you to rise and go down a desert road, do not be afraid. Though barren, the desert is the place of revelation. As you pass through, someone will draw near. It may be the risen Christ, disguised as a weary stranger. Behold the face of your God, and offer the stranger your water.

Sixth Sunday of Easter

Lections: Acts 10:44-48; Psalm 98; I John 5:1-6; John 15:9-17

Call to Worship
L: O sing a new song to the Lord our God, a song resounding to the ends of the earth!
P: A song of birth and gladness,
L: A song of life and peace!
P: A song of love and victory,
A: A song of faith and power!
L: O let your voices roar with the seas! Clap hands with the floods and shout with the hills!
A: For our blinded eyes are opened, and our deafened ears unstopped; our crippled feet are leaping, and our muted tongues have found their song![28]

Invocation. Mother of heaven, you have delivered us. You have brought us, like your child Jesus, from that world

---

[28] Inspired by Isaiah 35:5-6.

created and ruled by our parents, and ushered us into the world that you, alone, create and rule.

Love us, O Spirit, with the love that transforms the tomb into a womb. Let the waters of rebirth forever break upon your creation, that what is in heaven may be begotten on earth.

Litany

L: This cannot be! The Spirit of power has touched the unclean ones, whom we had shut outside the gate!

P: Shall we be amazed? The Lord our God has promised it!

L: This cannot be! The Spirit of love has invaded our enemies, whom we had stoned with spite and hate!

P: Shall we be amazed? The Lord our God has promised it!

L: Yes, this *can* be, for the Christ of God has greatly loved.

P: This *can* be, for in Christ we greatly love one another.

L: No greater love have we than this, that we should lay down our lives for a friend:

P: The unclean one outside our gate.

L: No greater love have we than this, that we should take up the cross for a friend:

P: The enemy stoned with spite and hate.

L: These things *shall* be, for the first heaven and earth have passed away, and we see them new, as the Lord has promised.[29]

P: Our God has come to dwell among us, and we have come to offer praise, for every tear is wiped away, and death shall be no more!

Prayer for One Voice. O Lord, your first group of followers was a motley lot. Fishermen, housewives, tax collectors, prostitutes, rebels, and more: some of them would have been mutual enemies had Christ not brought them together, and most would have walked through their lives indifferent to one another, for each had traveled a different road, and each had harbored different hopes. And yet in Christ their crowded ways crossed. Their lives intersected for all time.

---

[29] This and the following imagery is inspired by Revelation 21:1-5.

Now they were promised that the way of one would become the way of many, that the hope of one would become the hope of many.

O Lord, we are just as motley a lot. Some of us have had our differences, and many of us have been indifferent. We have traveled our own roads and harbored our own fears. And yet, in Christ, our crowded ways have crossed, intersecting for all time. And Christ has become for us, as for the first disciples, our way and our hope.

As your people, God, we are given a new identity. We become your servants, and we serve with gladness. But this is not all. You sent Christ among us with a new word, that we are *more* than servants. "No longer do I call you servants," he declared, "for the servant does not know what the master is doing; but I have called you friends, for all that I have heard from God, I have made known to you. You did not choose me, but I chose you."

Your child, Jesus Christ, *chooses* us, not as mere servants, but as friends; chooses us to know what we had never known before, to do what we had never done before, to be what we had never been before. He chooses us, not because we are worthy to be chosen, but because he serves the unworthy. He chooses us, not because we have been washed free of sin, but because he washes the feet of sinners. He chooses us, not because of our performance in the past, but because of his faith in our future.

He chooses us to be his friends. He makes us his equals, instilling in us the capacity for compassion, inspiring in us the spirit of understanding, and arousing in us the desire for action. He chooses us, saying, "Truly, truly, they who believe in me will also do the works that I do; and greater works than these will they do."[30]

This, then, is our new identity: Though we be the servants of God, we are the friends of Christ. This, then, is our new calling: to love one another even as we have been loved. This, then, is our new commandment: that we love our God with all our being, and our neighbors as ourselves. This, then, is

---

[30] See John 14:12.

our new life: for they who love are born of God. This, then, is our new faith: that they who are born of God have the victory. Through Christ we are the victors over differences, and over indifference. Through Christ we are victors over the world that crucifies its God! Through Christ we are victors over the grave!

Benediction. Lord, you chose us, that we might go where you would have us go and do what you would have us do. Send us with humility, courage, and, most of all, love. This world has much to learn about the miracles wrought by humility and the wonders worked by courage. But it has most to learn about the mysteries revealed by the gentle touch of love.

Seventh Sunday of Easter

Lections: Acts 1:15-17, 21-26; Psalm 1; I John 5:9-13; John 17:6-19

Call to Worship
L: Come to the birthplace, and we shall be one, even as parent and child are one.
P: We come to the God who gives us life, whose life in the world is borne by our labor.
L: Let us come singing, and we shall be one, even as melody and harmony are one.
P: We come to the God who gives us song, and to whose lead we lend our voices.
L: Let us come dancing, and we shall be one, even as rhythm and motion are one.
P: We come to the God who gives us dance, and to whose movements we adapt our step.
A: We come to the birthplace, and we shall be one. We come to our God: we shall be one!

Invocation. Lord, you know our hearts. As Guide, you would have us follow you to the ends of the earth, but you know that we hide in the corners of ourselves. As Teacher, you would have us discover you in the depths of our being, but

99

you know that we meditate on the surface of things. As Lover, you would have us pledge ourselves to you with an unbreakable vow, but you know that we wed ourselves to other gods.

Lord, you know our hearts. Guide, teach, and love them into knowing what they do not know about themselves, that they might become what you would have them be.

Litany

L: A seed sprang up from the earth, tended by a kindly hand.

P: Planted by a stream of water, it grew up straight and strong.

L: A tree sprang up and stood on earth;

P: And in its season it yielded fruit, with leaves that did not wither.

L: Yet an abundant yield and a hardy flower could not appease an angry world.

P: The rains scoffed and did not fall; the sun sinned and did not shine.

L: The soil laughed and did not feed; the wind blew and did not stop.

P: Its life fell into bitter hands, and soon the fruit it bore became thorns.

L: Its life fell down among tramping boots, and soon its hardy leaves wore purple.

P: Ashes to ashes, dust to dust, earth swallowed the tree as the sun died in the west.

L: But, now, see what springs forth again in the world: a hundred seeds sprout, a thousand trees rise!

P: By streams of water, let them grow; let them grow up straight and strong.

L: By streams of water, let them yield their fruit, and let their leaves not wither.

A: And may this world have learned to care. God, let our world learn to care.

Prayer for One Voice. O God, you sent a fragile, strong life into a strong, fragile world. That life grew, and he was called the

Lord of the Dance. But the world frowned upon the dance he danced and nailed his feet to a tree. That life grew, and he was called the Singer of the Song. But the world grimaced at the song he sang, and lifted vinegar to his lips. That life grew, and he was called the Ruler of Life. But the world scorned the life he lived and gambled away his purple robe.

O God, you sent a fragile, strong life. A screaming baby, he was wrapped in swaddling cloths and laid in a manger. A silent body, he was wrapped in linen cloths and laid in a tomb. He was like us, one day thrust into the world, one day thrust from it. The challenges that lay between his manger and his tomb were different from ours, but his mission was the same: to awaken to the knowledge that we are one with you; to awaken to the knowledge that we are brothers and sisters and you, our father and mother; to awaken to the knowledge that, in you and in one another, we shall find birth, life, and rebirth.

Just as the cloths in our manger are replaced by child's clothes, the shrouds in the tomb are not our final garments. In you we have life: a fragile yet strong life; a life capable of bearing the cross, confident that the cross will not have the last word; a life trembling as it enters the tomb, trusting that it will rise again; a life crucified, dead, buried, and resurrected on the third day, day after day after day.

In you, O God, we have life, not for our own sake, but for the sake of this world. As you sent Christ into the world to save it, so you send us. Strengthen our fragility, Lord, that we may not break. Weaken our strength, Lord, that we may not burst. For self-contempt and self-pride are the dragons on our daily road between manger and tomb, death and return.

Lord, tend our life that it may grow. And, if the world sees in us the Lord of the Dance, let it put away its hammer and nails and leap with us. If the world hears in us the Singer of the Song, let it spill its vinegar upon the ground and join our chorus. If the world feels in us the Ruler of Life, let it cast its dice into the sea and take with us the risk of faith.

For the sake of our world, O God, we dedicate our feet, our

101

lips, and our lives, that our world may be consecrated in truth and baptized in life.

Benediction. Risen Lord, you have ascended, but we remain. As you prayed that we should not be taken out of the world, send us into the world. Keep us one as we depart, and keep us faithful as we go.

Season After Pentecost

Pentecost

Lections: Acts 2:1-21; Psalm 104:24-34; Romans 8:22-27; John 15:26-27; 16:4*b*-15

Call to Worship

L: O World, come together in one place,
W: And suddenly an almighty roar shall sound:
M: The rush of a mighty wind,
A: A tempest from the mountaintop!
L: O World, kneel together in one place,
W: And suddenly a fiery pillar shall rise:
M: The tongue of a fiery spirit,
A: A flash from heaven's crown!
L: O World, come and kneel together:
A: And the place shall be sacred; the moment, divine!

Invocation. Spirit, we call! And many are the names by which we call you. You are Creator: father and mother. You are Provider: bread and wine. You are Counselor: guide and beacon. You are Helper: talent and will. You are Reconciler: bridge and the first step. You are Presence: host and guest.

Our names for you gush forth as waters from desert springs; they teem as creatures in the seas. Our God, who art in heaven, hallowed be thy names! Come to us, on earth as in heaven!

Litany

L: Long, Lord!
P: For so long, O Lord!
A: Long have we groaned with the universe!
L: Our eyes have shed the tears of the rain,
P: Our hearts have pitched the complaints of the thunder,
A: With only an inch of understanding, with only a minute of patience!

L: We have trusted for a step and doubted for a mile; we have hoped for a day and despaired for an age.

P: We have swapped your mountain for slippery slopes; we have traded forty days for an instant of pleasure.

A: For so long, O Lord!

L: But now your Spirit comes, to guide us into truth.

P: Your Spirit is pouring out; out it pours upon all flesh: It looks on the waters, and the world trembles; it touches the mountains, and their summits smoke!

A: Your Spirit rushes forth to baptize with fire!

L: Now we shall prophesy of things unseen and hope for things unheard. Our young shall have visions of heaven on earth, and our old shall dream dreams of things that will be:

P: Where once rain cried, a rainbow shall bend; where once thunder moaned, the songbird shall warble.

A: The Spirit explodes and floods the earth! O groanings, give birth to a cry of freedom! O lamentations, to ecstasy!

Prayer for One Voice. O wise and gracious God, how intimately you know the creation that your hand is fashioning, that breathes the wind of your spirit!

Though you have an infinite capacity to preserve, you have so designed creation that resurrection, not preservation, is the aim of all life. You have set the seasons turning in their cycle; you have set the earth spinning, circling the sun like an immortal lover.

All is change, all is motion: This is your will, that even in the endless red heat of the Sahara the sands will creep before the wind, and even over the endless blue ice of the Arctic the sun will sink before the stars. Since the beginning, evening has followed morning, and you have declared the day good.

This is the way of this world, for in the soil of your hand eternity is a flower, and in the ocean of your eye immortality is the tide. This you know, but we desire not change but permanence; not motion but repose; not evening and morning but eternal noon. We would use our freedom to protect what we have at this moment and to perpetuate who we are at this time.

O wise and gracious God, you create us in your image, but we hide it well. Your messenger, Jesus Christ, worked to awaken us to the holy temple within us, where the change and motion of death and resurrection receive your blessing. He died and arose as its crowning expression. But, predictably, when he had risen, we had difficulty recognizing him, because he was no longer the same. We would not believe, because he was different. When he was dead, we had wanted him back, we had longed for "the good old days." But his return brought a new day, and he was not back to stay.

We begged him not to go. But he replied that it was to our advantage that he leave; if he did not, the Spirit would not come. He knew that, if he remained, we would *use* him. He had walked his road; we would bronze his steps. He had preached the gospel; we would engrave it in stone. He had carried his cross; we would adore it as a relic. He had conquered the grave; we would kneel at the tomb. Jesus knew that, if he remained, he would forever be merely the focus of our wonder and the object of our worship—our excuse for looking to a past already gone instead of a future yet to come. We would preserve him instead of serving him. Eternal noon would be confined to Sunday morning. We would commit him to the tomb once again, and thereby banish our lives to the same fate.

Your messenger knew this, and so, despite our protests, he left us, that we might dwell in your Spirit—the spirit of wisdom and understanding, the spirit of counsel and might, the spirit of knowledge and awe[31]; the spirit that moved over the face of the waters in the beginning of time.[32]

O God, in our hands you have placed the seeds of the eternal flower. In the power of your Spirit, let us not hold them forever, but risk their planting. In our eyes you have placed droplets of the immortal tide. In the power of your Spirit, let us not keep them forever, but risk their running. For through the planting of the seed shall your kingdom

---

[31] Inspired by Isaiah 11:2.
[32] See Genesis 1:2.

grow, through the crying of the tear shall your seed flourish, and through dying and rising shall your people live.

Benediction

L: Spirit, steer us from our path of destruction into the way of life.

P: Sustain us as we go with the bread and the wine of the new world.

L: Guide us to your beacon,

P: Endowing our ability and inspiring our will.

L: Be our bridge over troubled waters and the step that moves our feet;

A: And be ahead of us, among us, and behind us until our journey's end.

Trinity Sunday
First Sunday After Pentecost

Lections: Isaiah 6:1-8; Psalm 29; Romans 8:12-17; John 3:1-17

Call to Worship

L: You in your fields! Come in to the barn, for the voice of the Lord cracks over the grain.

P: The skies are clapping their dappled hands and tramping upon the ground.

L: You in your boats! Come in to the shore, for the voice of the Lord breaks over the deep.

P: The floods are lifting up their voice[33] and pounding upon the strand.

L: You in your shops! Come down to the cellar, for the voice of the Lord whirls over the rooftops.

P: The winds are stripping the forests bare and shaking windows in their frames.

L: You in your fields, your boats and your shops, come into the temple where all shall cry, "Glory!"

A: Give glory to God, who thunders above! Give glory to God, who rumbles below! Give glory to God, from here to beyond!

---

[33] Inspired by Psalm 93:3.

Invocation. O Holy One, we enter your presence. Ahead of us a bush burns without leaving an ember; an angel stands without touching the ground. The bush may be just a tree bursting into brilliant flower, but the sight bewitches. The angel may be just a child swinging from its branches, but the vision entrances.

Your presence, O God, makes of this world a mystery; of this life, an odyssey. Illumine our shadowed world with your glory, that we might behold you in a world transformed.

Litany

L: How is it that when I whisper on the breeze, it is too loud to be heard? That when I trumpet in the thunder, no one can hear?

P: But here we are, Lord! Speak your word.

L: If you enter my presence, your bones may rattle. If you stand before me, your lips may stammer.

P: But here we are, Lord! Speak your word.

L: If I summon you here to send you forth, shall your heart falter? Shall your breath fail?

P: We are ready, Lord! Send us forth.

L: Then go, and say to my world, "You hear and hear, but do not understand; you see and see, but do not perceive."[34]

P: A grievous word, Lord! Must *we* pronounce it? Who are *we* that *we* should go?

L: Go, and say, "Your hearts shall grow fat, your ears shall grow heavy, your eyes shall drop in sleep; lest you see, and hear, and understand—"

P: How long, O Lord, must we bear such a word?

L: "—lest you turn from your ways and find your healing."

P: They will not believe, nor attend to our voice!

L: But here am I! Speak my word!

P: We are a people of bumbling tongues!

L: Here am I! Speak my word!

---

[34] This and the following quotes are taken from Isaiah 6:9-11.

P: Can you not let honey drip from our lips? Must you demand we be thorns in their flesh?

L: Here am I! I send you forth.

P: O Lord, we pray, send somebody else![35]

L: How long, my people, must *I* endure!

Prayer for One Voice. O One who is as no other, we dare to call upon your name, for you have revealed that we, like Christ, are one with you.[36] In you our bodies dwell; in you our spirits breathe; in you our minds explore. In you our births are begun, and our deaths, transformed. In you our hopes reside, and our fears are harbored.

We celebrate this, our oneness with you: As your daughters, we rise up; as your sons, we grow; as sisters and brothers of Christ, we discover our power and our vulnerability. But we must also confess that we have often celebrated this mysterious union while casting an uncertain glance over our shoulder.

Like Isaiah, we welcome your call—as long as you call us to pleasantries. Like Nicodemus, we seek your answers—as long as they conform to common logic. Like your earliest disciples, we hail every sign of your presence—as long as it satisfies our expectations.

So you see, Lord, while you say that we are one with you, we are not convinced. We are only willing to offer you *parts* of ourselves. You want us to jump in with both feet? We will put one foot in and keep one foot out. You want us to be single-minded? We will split every hair of every argument. You want us to commit our spirits? We will divide ourselves right down the middle, like the baby of Solomon's legend. You can have half, we say, and that will have to do.

But that does *not* do, does it? Even the most imaginative mathematician cannot cut oneness in two and still have one. Oneness simply *is*. We have no choice in the matter. It is not that you *prefer* us to *become* one with you; in Christ you have *demonstrated* that we *are* one with you.

---

[35] These and other "excuses" inspired by those put forth by Moses in Exodus 3–4.

[36] See John 17:11.

108

Are we too afraid to confess it, too stubborn to acknowledge it? Whatever the reason, we have shrunk from the truth, hiding in any corner of life that we could find, thinking that there you could not find us. But always you are there, because that is where *we* are.

"Truly, truly . . . unless one is born anew, one cannot see the kingdom of God." We must begin all over again, Lord. Teach us again how to see, but this time through *your* eyes. Teach us again to walk, this time in *your* shoes. Teach us again to feel, this time through *your* senses. Teach us again to love, this time with *your* heart.

O One, who is as no other yet one with all, help us to be born again. Inspire in us the confidence that you will be born with us, that you will grow with us. Then we shall surely perceive the kingdom where, before, we perceived only dust—in the world and in ourselves.

Benediction
L: Whom shall the Lord send?
P: The daughters and sons of God!
L: And who will go for the Lord?
P: The sisters and brothers of Christ!
L: *Who* will go for the Lord?
P: The people made one in the Spirit!
L: Let all the world shout, Glory to God!
P: Let all that *is* shout, Glory!

Sunday Between May 29 and June 4 Inclusive
(*if after Trinity Sunday*)

Lections: I Samuel 3:1-20; Psalm 139:1-6, 13-18; II Corinthians 4:5-12; Mark 2:23–3:6

Call to Worship
L: The God who answers in a day of trouble is among us,
P: And, behold, it is very good!
L: The God who lights a candle during the night is here,
P: And, behold, it is very good!
A: Hearts, rejoice! For peace has triumphed over trouble, and morning has broken eternal night!

109

Invocation. O God, you do not see as we see. You do not look upon us as we look upon others. Our eyes are seduced by outward appearance, but yours cut straight to the heart.

Search us, O God. Lay bare our ardent longing for you, and grant our heart's desire.

Litany
L: When a tattered stranger is wounded, and those around us tend the better-dressed:
M: Shall we be Law, an impatient toe tapping upon the floor?
W: Or shall we be Love, an able hand probing for a human pulse?
L: When a fragile spirit is shattered, and those around us will not pick up the pieces:
M: Shall we be Destruction, another empty bottle smashing against the wall?
W: Or shall we be Creation, old glass fragments being melted into something new?
L: When the defenseless earth is poisoned, and those around us hide from the hideous places:
M: Shall we be Silence, an unseen snake hissing before its strike?
W: Or shall we be Sound, a thunderstorm drenching a thirsty forest?
L: O Lord, whether body, spirit, or world requires healing, let us not withhold it. If the choice be ours, let love triumph over law.
A: If the choice be ours, let creation overcome destruction.
L: If the choice be ours, let sound resound through silence.
A: In the name of the tattered stranger, the fragile spirit and the defenseless earth, we pray.

Prayer for One Voice. Almighty God, what power you pour out upon us! What possibilities you instill within us! You fill our hearts, these fragile earthen pots, with strength and promise. A treasure, indeed, you bestow.

Yet we are tempted to hide it, to hoard it. While we

conserve our power for some rainy day, the powerless are consumed around us. While we preserve our potential for the day of destiny, the actual threatens us with the day of doom.

It is an old story, Lord, heard and told a hundred times. Yet we have not learned. We must still confess our resemblance to Eli, the cowardly chief priest of Israel, who knew of his sons' abuse of their priestly office but whose love of his position made him reluctant to discipline them. Like him, we rely less on your power than on our judgment. Our concern is less for your purpose than for our privilege.

We must also acknowledge our likeness to the Pharisees, whose authority was bound by a rigid religion. Like them, we depend less on your mercy than on our purity. Our loyalty is less to our neighbors than to our rules.

Remind us, O God, that Jesus Christ our Lord was a rule-breaker; that he called tax collectors as disciples, partied with sinners, and even healed people on the sabbath. Teach us that sometimes, like him, we may have to break human rules in fidelity to a higher law—the law of love. Remind us, too, that Jesus Christ stood against all authorities to proclaim that law, even unto death on a cross. Remind us lest we, like the Pharisees, should plot against truth; lest we, like Eli, should dishonor our calling.

Your purpose, O God, will not be thwarted. You have poured out your power upon us! You have instilled your possibilities within us! You have filled our hearts, these fragile earthen pots, with strength and promise. If some of us become misers and hoard the treasure you have placed within us, open the generous hearts of others and loose their treasures upon the earth. In the redemption of the world, let their treasures be returned to you a thousandfold.

Benediction. Return now to the world, and go gladly, despite your fears. Though afflicted, you will not be crushed; though perplexed, you will not be driven to despair; though lonely, you will not be forsaken. The Lord of life dwells in you and among you, now and forever.

LITANIES AND OTHER PRAYERS

Sunday Between June 5 and June 11 Inclusive
(if after Trinity Sunday)

Lections: I Samuel 8:4-20; 11:14-15; Psalm 138; II Corinthians 4:13–5:1; Mark 3:20-35

Call to Worship
L: Let us lift up the name of our God!
P: Let us praise the faithfulness of the Lord!
L: For just as the Lord's greatness fills the heavens,
P: The Lord's love embraces the earth,
L: Preserving our life in the midst of trouble.
A: Let us give thanks to the Lord our God!

Invocation. We turn to you, O Lord, for we have learned the folly of putting our trust in earthly rulers. They promise peace with justice for our children, yet they take them from us and make them run before war's chariots. Now, O Lord, we put our trust in you, assured that, if we seek your justice, we will receive it; that, if we seek your peace, we shall find it—a peace other rulers can neither give nor take away.

Litany
L: Yesterday I would have cried for God, but I did not know God's name. The scribes insisted that it could not be written; the sages, not be said.
P: But now the world has changed. Cry to God, and call him, "Father!" Cry to God, and call her, "Mother!"
A: The name shall be revealed by the lips of your heart, and God shall answer.
L: Yesterday I would have appealed to *you,* but I did not know your names. Your shifting eyes told me to keep my distance; your upraised hands, to stay away.
P: But now *we* have changed. Appeal to us, and call us, "Brothers!" Appeal to us, and call us, "Sisters!"
A: Our names shall be revealed by the lips of your heart, and we shall answer.
L: Today life has changed, for God is near.
P: Life has changed, for we are near one another.

112

L: Behold, salvation comes—to me, and to all!

P: Behold, liberation is here—for the one and the many!

L: O God, my father and my friend—

P: Our mother and our savior—

A: The hands of this family are clasped together, and still the circle grows! May love endure for all generations!

Prayer for One Voice. O God, hear our prayer! We need to know that, beyond us, you are. For while we seek our own salvation, it cannot be had through striving. We think highly of ourselves, O Lord, but we are not great—only driven by dreams of greatness. And we have stumbled upon such dreams until finally we have fallen and plunged into the pit.

We cannot see; the midnight-dark steals our sight. We cannot breathe; the stale air smothers our breath. We cannot hear; our pounding heart deafens our ears. We cannot bear it. For here, in the pit, we meet our demons, our fiercest enemies, our terrible idols—things seen substituted for things unseen; things fleeting worshiped in place of things eternal. Here, in the pit, the fact of our baseness explodes the myth of our greatness. Here, in the pit, we stand alone.

And yet, O God, we are not alone. For suddenly we perceive that we are cowering in the midst of lions. These are the royal powers upon which we may call—powers you have set within us to prey upon the demons and consume the false gods. Give us courage in their presence; let us trust them. By devouring all within us that is not yours, they shall carry us up and out of the pit.

Yes, Lord, we shall be saved! Reveal to us our potential for evil and for good, that the pit might become the crest of your mountain, and our fall, a fall upward to you!

Benediction. Do not lose heart, for *there* is the abode of God. If your heart be troubled, God will share your agony; if your heart be triumphant, God will share your gladness. Do not lose heart, for *there* is the shelter for your neighbors. May you share *their* agony and gladness, as you trek, arm-in-arm, to the mountaintop.

113

Sunday Between June 12 and June 18 Inclusive
(if after Trinity Sunday)

Lections: I Samuel 15:34–16:13; Psalm 20; II Corinthians 5:6-17; Mark 4:26-34

Call to Worship
L: Some boast of tanks and guns, and put their trust in planes and missiles.
P: Fear not! They who trust in arms will collapse and fall. The Lord does wondrous things!
L: Others boast of justice and mercy, and put their trust in the Lord their God.
P: Take heart! They who trust in God will arise and stand tall. The Lord does wondrous things!
L: Therefore, we will not fear, though our rulers betray us;
P: We will shout for joy, for the Lord is God!
A: Come, let us bless the Lord our God, who alone does wondrous things!

Invocation. O Creator of this world, of every world that was or is or shall ever be, do not abandon us. Though our hands work harm and our lips speak lies, though we betray you with body and soul, do not forsake us.

Weep over us as Samuel wept over the death of the demented Saul, that paragon of virtue who became the embodiment of evil. Weep over us as Jesus wept over the dying of the decadent Jerusalem, the holy city that became the killer of prophets.[37] Weep over us, and bless us, our Creator and our Redeemer.

Litany
L: How precious is human life!
P: How precious, human love!
L: With life comes death, the sweet release;
P: With love comes pain, the sweet remembrance.
L: There is no life that has no death coursing through its veins;
P: There is no love that has no pain running through its heart.

---

[37] See Matthew 23:37 f.

L: So let us press our common pulse, quickening enemy and friend—

P: For that pulse is our lifeline and the heartbeat of God.

L: Let us join hands with our joy, made bright by the shadow of death;

P: And let us embrace our grief, made dark by the glory of life.

L: Let us reach toward our ecstasy, made high by the depth of pain;

P: And let us bend toward our despair, made deep by the height of love.

L: For we know that where there is joy and grief, God shall be the sweet release;

P: And where there is ecstasy and despair, Christ shall be the remembrance sweet.

Prayer for One Voice. Awakener of dreams and Revealer of visions, reveal yourself to our hibernating spirits and awaken us from our sleep. Long have we snuggled in secret places, shut off from any new sign of spring. Long have we slumbered through the winters of the soul, wrapped in an apathy that seeks only to be forgotten; frozen in an indifference that seeks only to be sheltered.

This is the eternal winter that chills our nerve and hardens our heart. Our memory of spring soon fades, and we cease expecting her approach. We no longer await the thaw of the earth, the warmth of the sun, or the bud of the flower, for there is nothing for which to hope. We become those who walk by sight, not by faith; and because the sight of deepest winter is not pleasing to our eyes, we soon do not walk at all.

O Lord, arouse in our dormant hearts a vision of the springtime, when the old has passed away and the new has come; when the bitter cold has fled before the sun, and the whipping wind has died before a breeze, and the forgotten flower has opened in morning dew. For while the world sleeps, the silent sower sows the seeds, and no frost nips their blossoms. These are the mysterious seeds of the kingdom, yielding the flower of faith and the blossom of righteousness.

Awaken us, O God, to this sweet scent that plays at the

nostril. This rich, upturned earth awaits its planting; plant your seeds, and we shall tend them. Scatter your seeds, and we shall baptize them. Tuck them into good soil, and we shall pluck the weeds. Multiply them, and we shall harvest. The bounty of that harvest shall be your joy, and its plenty shall be our hope. For as the seasons of the field change, so too the seasons of the heart; and where once there was winter, now there is spring.

Benediction. The love of Christ constrains us. In the staying power of the Lord, we find the courage to dream. Therefore, let us dream passionately. In the abiding will of the Lord, we find the determination to act. Therefore, let us act resolutely. In the enduring spirit of the Lord, we find the grace to persevere. Therefore, let us persevere boldly.

Sunday Between June 19 and June 25 Inclusive
(*if after Trinity Sunday*)

Lections: I Samuel 17:4-11, 19-23, 32-49; Psalm 9:9-20; II Corinthians 6:1-13; Mark 4:35-41

Call to Worship
L: The Spirit drifts over the face of the deep, and though the wind rises and the sea swells, the Spirit is at rest.
P: Let us worship the Spirit in silence, for a voice upon the water whispers, "Be still, and know that I am God."[38]
L: The Spirit leads us from chaos to calm, and though we fear the wind and dread the sea, the Spirit restores our souls.[39]
P: Let us worship the Spirit in strength, for a voice upon the water speaks, "Be not afraid; it is I."

Invocation. O God, how often have we meditated upon your steadfast love! Our speech has been reduced to silence by your measureless grace. Our reverence has been lifted to revelry by your boundless joy.

If it is because of your love that we can serve, because of

---

[38] See Psalm 46:10.
[39] Inspired by Psalm 23:2-3.

your grace that we can forgive, and because of your joy that we can rejoice, be present among us. And like the wind and the sea, who obey your voice, we shall grow calm and yield to your power.

Litany
L: Today is the day of our salvation!
P: Now is the time for reconciliation!
L: The stronghold of God is established on earth;
P: Let our hands be its streets; our hearts, its habitations.
L: Let us not cower in our ghettos, awaiting a greater word.
P: In our lives are many rooms; let us prepare a place for the Lord our God.[40]
L: Let us prepare the way,
P: Lest the sun set upon our hesitation, and we bequeath to our children the world's destruction.
L: Let us prepare *now*,
P: Lest the moment slip past our busyness, and we leave a legacy of indifference.
L: Let tomorrow live,
P: That God may save!
L: Let the future *be*,
P: That we may reconcile!
A: For the stronghold of God is established on earth, and it shall not be moved!

Prayer for One Voice. O God, yours is the work of creation, of inspiration, of striking a spark in the darkness, of carving a figure from stone. Yours is the work of transformation, of change, of luring a spring from winter, of coaxing a day from night. Yours is the work of reconciliation, of union, of bonding humanity and nature, of joining human to human.

You reveal yourself to us as the One who creates, transforms, and reconciles, and for no small purpose. In so doing, you reveal to us: ourselves. Made in your image, ours too is revealed to be the work of creation, transformation, and reconciliation.

No small responsibility. You have placed in our hands our

---
[40] Inspired by John 14:2-3.

own generation, and the next and the next as well. Perhaps in the ancient world it was enough for one of your servants to ask, "Am I my brother's keeper?" But that question today is dwarfed by our world. Today not only the brother, but the sister; not only the sister, but the friend; not only the friend, but the enemy; not only the enemy, but the unnamed; not only the unnamed, but the unborn; not only the unborn, but the unforeseen—all generations of peoples, creatures, and worlds are in our hands. And somehow, in your great hope and even greater mercy, you can acknowledge this and still say to us, "Behold, I see what I have made, and it is good."

O Lord, we fear that our hands shall tremble; we are terrified by the task you have given us. We are poor caretakers of this world. We have ravaged our lands, and still we plunder; we have defiled our seas, and still we pollute; we have poisoned our air, and still we discharge. And now we are shuttling off into space, toward unknown worlds, as if we were fleeing from our own destruction.

O God, if we are to be creators, give us the drive to create life, rather than death. If we are to be transformers, give us the power to transform the ugly into the beautiful, rather than the beautiful into the ugly. If we are to be reconcilers, give us the compassion to reconcile for peace and justice, rather than for truce and power. If, O God, we are to do your work in the midst of and on behalf of our brother and our sister, our friend and our enemy, the unnamed and the unborn and the unforeseen, we can do so only because of who *you* are, and who we can become through faith in you.

Benediction. Make strong our hearts, O God, these doorways to your city. Then, when the armies of this world assemble at our gate, when the fears and fates meet to conspire our ruin, they shall be astounded. In an instant, they shall panic; in a moment, they shall scatter. For we shall stand before them in faith, as if stilling the winds upon the sea!

Sunday Between June 26 and July 2 Inclusive

Lections: II Samuel 1:17-27; Psalm 130; II Corinthians 8:7-15; Mark 5:21-43

Call to Worship

L: If you hunger in your wilderness, come, and manna shall fall from heaven, this bread that the Lord has given.[41]

P: Loaves and fishes shall fill the baskets, this bread that Christ has broken.[42]

L: Let us take and eat, that our world may find healing;

P: Let us partake at one table, that our world may know peace.

L: Let us bless and break our bread together,

P: That those who gather much may have nothing over,

A: And those who find crumbs may have no lack.

Invocation. O Lord our God, your love falls on your creatures like morning dew. Therefore, we beseech you, grant to us the fullness of faith, that we might invest one another with trust. Breathe to us the full utterance of your word, that we might address one another with understanding. Bring us to the full knowledge of your salvation, that we might liberate one another with truth. Arouse in us the full earnestness of your power, that we might uphold one another with strength. And surround us with the fullness of your love, that we might embrace one another with compassion.

Litany

L: A child lay somewhere close to death. Will someone please rush to her side?

P: All the crowd is filled with laughter; every street is choked with scorn.

L: Some people shrug and turn away, leaving the child unto its fate.

P: Some lie in wait for the one who will go, the charge of "Blasphemy!" fat on their tongues.

L: Will anyone's faith uplift a daughter?

P: Will anyone's hope restore a son?

L: Without our love, the children will languish.

---

[41] See Exodus 16:14 f.
[42] See Matthew 14:15 f.

119

P: Without our boldness, the children will die.

L: Without our presence, the children will leave us,

P: Without our touch, they will not awake.

L: O God, let mercy prevail over fear, that someone lost may soon be found;

A: O, let life break through the dream of death, that the one asleep may soon arise!

Prayer for One Voice. O God, we look to you this day for signs of your presence. We do not doubt that you are here, for there is no place where you are not. We doubt, rather, that your presence can alter the circumstances of our present. You are unseen, but our loyalty is to the seen. We trust things more than we trust people; we have more faith in people than we have in you. For things and people are familiar, and noticeable, while the movements of your Spirit are strange and subtle. Things and people—we believe that we can control them; but your Spirit—it blows where it wills, and we do not know whence it comes or whither it goes.[43]

And so, O God, we request a sign, some simple epiphany. We do not demand it, for we stand on holy ground; our feet are bare and unclean, and no hands but yours can wash them.

We are not alone in our request. The Israelites built the ark of the covenant, wherein your Spirit might dwell. They *knew* that your presence filled its space; they believed so absolutely, we are told, that whoever brushed against its gilded wood—the house of the living God—fell dead. The ark was *their* sign, but it was of their making, and carried with it life and death.

The crowds demanded signs of Jesus. But they scoffed when the wonders were not great enough; they envied when the wonders were too great; they threatened when the wonders appeared in the wrong place or at the wrong time or to the wrong people. Healings were *their* signs—a crippled hand made straight, a blind eye made seeing—but the signs

---

[43] See John 3:8.

120

had to be of *their* design; and thus, their demands carried with them less life than death.

And the death of the healer was their ultimate demand. The death of your supreme sign, O God; we clamored for his crucifixion. O Lord, we want your sign, but you know that on one day we shall celebrate it, and on the next, we shall kill it. If you send us prophets, we shall slander them, stone them, shoot them, crucify them. If you send us liberators, we shall blame them, betray them, break them and bury them. If you send us signs, O Lord, we shall ignore them or imitate them or injure them or idolize them—but we shall not receive them as you receive us.

Dear God, we cannot request a sign. But request it we must, for little is our faith. Appear among us, and unveil our eyes that we might see you. Speak to us, and unstop our ears that we might hear you. Enlighten us, and illumine our minds that we might understand you. Embrace us, and open our hearts that we might care—before it is too late. Through our little faith in that which is seen and heard and understood and felt, we shall find the fullness of faith in you.

Benediction. In this place your healing has begun. Now begins the healing of the world. Go in peace.

Sunday Between July 3 and July 9 Inclusive

Lections: II Samuel 5:1-5, 9-10; Psalm 48; II Corinthians 12:2-10; Mark 6:1-13

Call to Worship
L: We erect high altars and raise high steeples, but in no one place shall God be found.
P: We sing right hymns and preach right doctrines, but in no one word shall God be bound.
L: Our God is not bound, but our God shall build:
P: Not temples but truth, not shrines but *shalom*.
L: Our God is not bound, but our God shall build:
P: Not rituals but rights, not dogmas but dreams.

A: Not a space we call sacred, not a time we call holy, shall confine the works of the almighty Lord! Let us burst our bonds and break into praise, for our God is free: Our God is free!

Invocation. O Great Revealer, we come seeking visions. We come desiring dreams. Grant our wish: wave before us one branch of paradise lost, and we shall see in its leaf our life regained. Or conjure up a carpenter whose hands are as rough as the bark of a tree, and we shall behold in his face our salvation. Lift us, we plead, in a flight not of fancy, but of faith; not that we might boast of your presence, but that we might know your forgiveness.

Litany

L: I am the One who gives you life. Forever shall I be your God, and you shall be my people.

P: And if we have no royal blood, but sweat each day for bread?

L: I will be parent to your child; your child shall be my own.

P: And if our skin be a different shade, or our speech a stranger's tongue?

L: I will be parent to your child; your child shall be my own.

P: If we pray to another name, or worship you in another way?

L: I will be parent to your child; your child shall be my own.

P: If our body be afflicted, or our spirit be distressed?

L: I will be parent to your child; your child shall be my own.

P: If we die while yet alive, or slip beyond the door of death?

L: I will be parent to your child; your child shall be my own.

P: You are the One who gives us life; you are the One who gives us hope.

A: Forever shall you be our God, and we shall be your people!

Prayer for One Voice. O God of all, we rest in the knowledge that wherever we are, there shall you be also. Whether we reside in the palace of a king or the house of a carpenter; the mansion of a president or the dwelling of a tenant: ours is your dwelling-place. Whether we labor in the seat of a government or the assembly line of a factory; in the classroom of a school or the ward of a hospital: ours is your workplace. And even if our home be the street, and the door of the workplace be barred, ours is your resting place.

You are with us always, for yours is a loyalty that surpasses the greatest love we have ever known. It is a loyalty that persists through all terrors; survives, despite all betrayals; and endures, for all generations. Greater love has no one than this: you have laid down your love for the life of the world.

Let this loyalty of yours—so unknown, so strange—arouse in us a commitment to envision more, to do more, to be more. And not "more" only, but more *for you*. Give us the courage to surrender to you our weakness, that you might make it our strength. Grant us the humility to yield to you our power, that you might fill it with grace. And endow us with the confidence to submit to you our will, that you might adapt it to your purpose.

Our commitment to you shall render us unknown, shall make us strangers among many who once knew us. They will remember us in old roles, with old habits and haunts. The more we envision the kingdom, the more they will call us back to the "real" world. The more we do the work of the kingdom, the more their eyebrows will wrinkle. The more we *are* the kingdom, the more they will long for the persons we once were.

O God of all, we rest in the knowledge that wherever we are, there shall you be also. But that place where we dwell together—the kingdom of heaven on earth—is not an easy place in which to dwell. Help us to understand that our identity and mission must not depend on the acceptance of those who do not understand; that its success or failure must never be measured in human terms.

Benediction. Paradise shimmers in our midst; the highest heaven lies hidden all around us. Go, and you will discover God; and where you discover God most utterly, you shall know yourself most fully, and love your neighbor most perfectly.

Sunday Between July 10 and July 16 Inclusive

Lections: II Samuel 6:1-5, 12b-19; Psalm 24; Ephesians 1:3-14; Mark 6:14-29

Call to Worship
L: We gather in the name of Jesus Christ, the head of the church and the Savior of the world,
P: Not because we have invited Christ into our house, but because Christ has invited us into the house of the Lord.
L: We have come, not to tell Christ what we *will* do,
P: But to learn from Christ what we *must* do.
L: We have listened for the voice of the Lord in the earthquake, wind, and fire.
A: Now we await the still small voice. Speak, O Lord, for your servants hear.

Invocation. O God, you have created us for yourself. You have made our minds restless until they embrace your purpose as our own; our hearts aimless, until they adopt your will as our own; and our hands profitless, until they seize your task as our own. We praise you in the name of Jesus Christ our Lord, in whom you have revealed the person you created us to be. Let your revelation never cease until our minds and hearts and hands are wholly committed to your service.

Litany
L: Let us praise the Lord in the house of the Lord!
P: Let us praise the house of the Lord for its faithful witness.
L: Let us celebrate its power to convict sinners of their guilt,
P: Moving them to confess the errors of their way.
L: Let us celebrate its power to convince prophets of the truth,
P: Empowering them to declare the word of the Lord.

L: Let us celebrate its power to alert stewards to their mission,

P: Equipping them to discern the humanity of the deprived.

L: Let us celebrate its power to turn disciples to their task,

P: Prompting them to join the ministry of healing.

L: Let us celebrate its power to recruit champions of the wronged,

P: Inspiring them to take up the cause of justice.

A: Let us praise the Lord in the house of the Lord! May our witness be faithful and our service, glad!

Prayer for One Voice. O God, you have created us for yourself and for one another in a world of your own making. You are Lord above all lords and God above all gods; and you are our Lord and our God. You are the light unto our path; were it not for you, we would dwell in deep darkness. You are the strength of our life; were it not for you, we could not resist the powers of evil. You are the hope of our tomorrows; were it not for you, we would break under the load of our yesterdays.

As we bow before you, dear Lord, refresh our memories. Let us not forget where we are, whose we are, or what the reason for our gifts. Remind us that the land in which we dwell, wherever it be, is your land; that the people among whom we dwell, whoever they be, are your people; and that the gifts with which we are endowed, whatever they be, are bestowed to make us one in our worship of you and our service to one another.

We have repeatedly affirmed these elementary truths of our faith. Yet we confess, O Lord, that only rarely have we made them the truths of our lives. We have treated the land as if we were not its stewards but its owners. We have dealt with other people as if our relationships were of no concern to you. And we have handled our gifts as if they were intended to set people apart rather than bring them together.

We thank you, dear Lord, for your gift of these precious truths of faith and for all those who have sought to teach us their importance. For our disregard of their teaching, we ask

125

your forgiveness. And we pray that you will give us hearts so attuned to your will that we will proceed to do it.

Remind us of our responsibility toward those who look to us for guidance. Let us not greet this responsibility with excuses. Save us from the temptation to exaggerate our inadequacies and our obstacles. Let us dwell, instead, on your mighty acts wrought through people of equally unpromising circumstances—the slaves in Egypt, the harp player from Bethlehem, the Carpenter from Nazareth, the tentmaker from Tarsus. As we ponder the lives of those who shaped our faith, we see people who looked not within or around but up. They gave up the inward look, anxiously trying accurately to assess their strengths and weaknesses. They gave up the outward look, nervously trying to separate their friends from their foes. And they adopted the upward look, faithfully seeking to conform their will to yours.

O God, you have commanded us to do unto others what we would have them do unto us. Enable us to give unto others the greatest gift others have given us. Face to face with the tensions within, troubles without, and threats on every side, help us follow the example of those who turned neither inward nor outward but upward. When our neighbors ask us for guidance, let us introduce them to our Guide.

Benediction. O God, as you have brought us together in this place to ponder the mind of Christ, send us back into the marketplace to do his bidding. When we open our lips, let it be to speak your truth; when we open our hearts, let it be to spread your love; and when we open our hands, let it be to proclaim your welcome.

Sunday Between July 17 and July 23 Inclusive

Lections: II Samuel 7:1-14*a*; Psalm 89:20-37; Ephesians 2:11-22; Mark 6:30-34, 53-56

Call to Worship
L: The Lord has restored our fortunes.

126

P: Come, you thankful people, come; let us rejoice and be glad!

L: The Lord has brought us near, a people once far off.

P: Come, you thankful people, come; let us rejoice and be glad!

L: The Lord has reconciled us in one body through the cross.

P: Come, you thankful people, come; let us rejoice and be glad!

A: Now we all have access to God in one spirit; let us rejoice and be glad!

Invocation. You, O Lord, are the Good Shepherd. Yet we drift like sheep *without* a shepherd. We pursue goals that demand too little of us, challenge too few of us, and threaten all of us. Deliver us from our aimless wanderings, O Lord, and lead us into paths of righteousness for your sake and ours.[44]

Litany

L: As we come together, we are pushed by our desire for success and pulled by Christ's summons to service.

P: Help us, dear Lord, to resist the push for success.

L: We desire a life of ease and privilege.

P: Help us, dear Lord, to resist the push for success.

L: We covet the power of fame and wealth.

P: Help us, dear Lord, to resist the push for success.

L: Yet we also esteem the call to duty and charity.

P: Help us, dear Lord, to heed the pull of service.

L: We lament the rule of hate and jealousy.

P: Help us, dear Lord, to heed the pull of service.

L: Above all, we long to do your will on earth as in heaven.

A: Help us, dear Lord, to heed your summons in the spirit of Christ.

Prayer for One Voice. O God, your glory fills heaven and earth; your creation is greater than our powers to describe. We are

---

[44] Inspired by Psalm 23:3.

your creatures; and you, our Creator. Who are we that you are mindful of us?[45] The distance between us could not be bridged from our side to yours; so you bridged it from your side to ours. Despite our disregard for you, our contempt for your law, and our violation of your covenant, in Jesus Christ you took upon yourself our human frame. In him you assumed all the limits and braved all the risks of every person born of earth. In him you became a member of our family that we might become members of your family. In him you turned our adoring eyes from the majesty of creation to the love of the Creator. For this, the mightiest of all your mighty acts, we worship you.

We thank you, dear Lord, that in Jesus you rejected our low opinion of human nature: for laying bare our preference for crowns over crosses; and for exposing our habit of sacrificing the joy of eternity for the pleasure of the moment. When we behold ourselves in him, we cannot but exclaim that you have made us little less than God and crowned us with glory and honor.[46]

But when we look away from him to ourselves, we behold a very different creature. We see a king shamelessly pursuing his ambition, ignoring the traditions of his people, to build a great temple. We discover that the enemy we most have to fear is the enemy within: that in our hearts there lurks a breaker of all those commandments designed to protect our neighbors from ourselves. The sight of this demon disgusts us, but we do not have to surrender to its power. Help us, dear Lord, so to fix our hearts upon Christ, that the good we *would*, we *do;* and the evil we would *not,* we *do not.*[47]

O God, our towns are full of people like the crowds that flocked to Jesus—sheep without a shepherd. Yet we know to which flock they belong, for we know who their shepherd is. Lead us to them, that we might lead them to you: that we and they might become one flock; that you might be the Good

---

[45] See Psalm 8:4.
[46] See Psalm 8:5.
[47] See Romans 7:15-20.

Shepherd of us all; and that, with singleness of mind and purity of heart, we might heed your voice.

Benediction. O God, who longs to continue in us the work begun in Jesus, let us who have been reconciled by Christ become reconcilers for Christ. Send us who have found peace in God's house to make peace in God's world.

Sunday Between July 24 and July 30 Inclusive

Lections: II Samuel 11:1-15; Psalm 14; Ephesians 3:14-21; John 6:1-21

Call to Worship
L: We do not come before you, O God, as heroes and heroines, making boasts and seeking halos.
P: We come before you as rebels and sinners, making confession and seeking forgiveness.
L: Like King David, we have exalted you in public, but we have betrayed you in secret.
P: Yet you have blotted out our transgressions, and you have forgiven our sins.
A: Open our mouths, O God, that we might shout your praise and hail your love.

Invocation. Almighty and everlasting God, you know that we are sinners, yet you treat us as if we were not; you know that we are unworthy of your love, yet you treat us as if we were. We thank you for welcoming us into your presence. We bow before you in confidence, not because of our goodness, but because of your grace. We pray that you will repeat in us the miracle you have worked in others—converting worshipers into witnesses and believers into disciples.

Litany
L: Let us remember all your sheep, O Lord, those of this fold and those not of this fold,
P: Lest we forget that you are the Good Shepherd of all.

L: When they worship you by other names, let us remember that you have not left yourself without witnesses in any place,[48]

P: Lest we forget that you are the Good Shepherd of all.

L: When they define goodness by other standards, let us remember that you turned a lecherous monarch into a righteous king,

P: Lest we forget that you are the Good Shepherd of all.

L: When they perpetrate deeds of utter selfishness, let us remember that you judge the thoughts of *our* hearts as well as the deeds of *their* hands,[49]

P: Lest we forget that you are the Good Shepherd of all.

L: When they express mindless prejudice, let us remember the log in our eyes before condemning the speck in theirs,[50]

P: Lest we forget that you are the Good Shepherd of all.

L: When they commit crimes of wanton violence, let us remember that you alone can separate the goats from the sheep,[51]

P: Lest we forget that you are the Good Shepherd of all.

A: Grant us, O Lord, by whatever name we call you, so to live in your love, that we may be united in your service.

Prayer for One Voice. Eternal and gracious God, whose standards reflect your goodness and who does not wink at their disregard, we adore you for your character and integrity. We stand in awe of your righteousness and of your lofty expectations, but we would not have it otherwise. Nothing so reassures us as the knowledge that you, our maker, are also our judge; that, if your demands are high, it is because you know that we are capable of meeting them; that, when you send prophets among us for our correction, it is not to assert your authority but to preserve our humanity; and that, even when we treat you with disrespect, you continue to respect us. We thank you, dear Lord, not only for

---

[48] See Acts 14:17.
[49] See Matthew 5:21 f.
[50] Inspired by Matthew 7:5.
[51] See Matthew 25:31-46.

130

your faith in us, but for your faithfulness toward us. We thank you for raising up prophets to rebuke us for our evil deeds, even as the psalmist confronted Israel.

Yet we must confess that the prophets of our time do not fare much better than the prophets of antiquity. We may not kill them as did the ancients, but neither do we crown them with halos. We cry out for them boldly to declare the will of the Lord. However, as soon as they begin to express opinions contrary to our own, we begin to question their credentials. If they call for an end to the arms race, we accuse them of abandoning tough minds for tender hearts. If they call for an end to racism, we accuse them of replacing realism with idealism. If they call for applying the brakes to nationalism, we accuse them of trading history for utopia. If they call for a war on poverty, we accuse them of sacrificing ambition for equality. If they call for the rehabilitation of criminals, we accuse them of defending the villains instead of the victims.

Forgive us, O God, for our response to our prophets. We may sometimes be right in questioning their solutions, but we are not right in ignoring the problems to which they point. Their remedies may not always be the best, but the wrongs they address are real. So we repent, O God, for thinking and for acting as if we could get rid of our problems by discrediting those who call them to our attention: for fragmenting your family, and for neatly separating the sheep from the goats, the innocent from the guilty, and the villains from the victims.

Help us, O God, to realize that we live in a world much too dangerous for such uncharitable attitudes. Help us see that we cannot remake the world, save as you, through Christ, have remade us: by living for you, dying unto self, and loving the undeserving. Give us the will so to enflesh this vision that we will make the world safe for your prophets—ready to grant that, if you be for them, we dare not be against them.

Benediction. O Lord, as we go forth to meditate on the story of the loaves and the fishes, let us not dwell on how much Jesus was able to do with so little. Neither let us dwell on how little we do with so much. Dismiss us, instead, with the desire to put ourselves, as Jesus did, wholly at your bidding.

Sunday Between July 31 and August 6 Inclusive

Lections: II Samuel 11:26–12:13*a*; Psalm 51:1-12; Ephesians 4:1-16; John 6:24-35

Call to Worship
L: In vain, O God, we have sought satisfaction in the things of space and time.
P: Now we come to seek fulfillment in your acts of mercy and grace.
L: Jesus said, "I am the bread of life; whoever comes to me shall not hunger, and whoever believes in me shall never thirst."
P: We come to you, Lord; give us to eat. We believe in you, Lord; give us to drink.

Invocation. O God, the source of peace in a world of turmoil, the fount of unity in a world of diversity, the oasis of meaning in a world of confusion, we turn to you for refuge. Grant us the peace that stills troubled waters, the unity that baptizes strange tongues and the meaning that blossoms in the desert, that we may joyfully praise you with our words and with our lives.

Litany
L: Come, children of God, listen to me and learn my ways.
P: Teach us your ways, Lord, and we shall walk in them.
L: I ache with those who feel pain; when my people suffer, I hearken to their cry.
P: Teach us your ways, Lord, and we shall walk in them.
L: I hunger with those who lack food; when my people faint, I listen to their plea.
P: Teach us your ways, Lord, and we shall walk in them.
L: I flounder with those who cannot read; when my people stumble, I give ear to their need.
P: Teach us your ways, Lord, and we shall walk in them.

L: I weep with those who have no friends; when my people despair, I attend to their plight.

P: Teach us your ways, Lord, and we shall walk in them.

L: I hurt with those who are estranged; when my people grieve, I answer their lament.

P: Teach us your ways, Lord, and we shall walk in them.

L: My eyes are toward the good, but I do not spare the righteous. My eyes are against the evil, but I do not hate the wicked.

A: As the heavens are high above the earth, your ways are higher than ours.[52] But teach us your ways, Lord, and we shall walk in them.

Prayer for One Voice. O God, you have created us to depend on one another; if we do not work together, we will tear the world apart. You have made us debtors to those who have gone before us; if we do not learn from them, we will cripple the world for those who will come after us. You have bestowed on us gifts to make us one; if we do not share them, we will not reach the better world toward which you would lead us. We praise you for entrusting us with so great a responsibility.

If only our faith were as great as your trust! But our record, at best, has been spotted. Instead of depending on others to work for the good of all, we have simply neglected them. Instead of learning from the experiences of previous generations, we have simply repeated them. Instead of distributing your gifts according to need, we have simply hoarded them.

For this betrayal of you, we ask your forgiveness, O God. Not only have we betrayed you as a people; we have betrayed you as individuals. Each of us has worked to delay the coming of your rule to earth. We know the power of lies to hurt, yet we have let gossip go unchecked. We know the power of silence to scar, yet we have left the truth unspoken. We know the power of prejudice to distort, yet

---

[52] Inspired by Isaiah 55:9.

we have let bigotry go unchallenged. We know the power of selfishness to seduce, yet we have let its grip go untested. True, we have not committed *all* the evils we deplore, but neither have we condemned them. We choose to be eye-winkers rather than whistle-blowers: to play it safe rather than straight; to promote harmony rather than justice; to heed the will of our neighbors rather than the word of our Lord.

We pray for mercy, O Lord, for having squandered our opportunities for bringing your rule to earth. And we pray not only for the release of our neighbors from the influence of our example, but for our own transformation: that, henceforth, when they do as we do, they will also be doing as we say; and that we and they might work together to turn your gifts into the foundation of that better world for which we pray.

Benediction. O Lord, we have gathered together to receive your counsel and discern your will. As we part, let us not go as we came. Let us leave with memories rekindled and hopes awakened. Help us so to heed your words that we will walk in your ways.

Sunday Between August 7 and August 13 Inclusive

Lections: II Samuel 18:5-9, 15, 31-33; Psalm 130; Ephesians 4:25–5:2; John 6:35, 41-51

Call to Worship
L: Let us sing a hymn in unison,
P: For we are not many, but one!
L: Let us praise our God in harmony,
P: For we are not one, but many.
L: Members are we, one of another: the body of Christ, the people of God:
P: Let our melody rise as if from one voice, while the chorus swells from each mouth of creation.

Invocation. O God, at our birth you thrust us into new worlds;

during the span of our years you deliver us into new life; and at our death you receive us unto still another new journey. O Creator, Deliverer, and Comforter, in you we place our trust, and we gratefully acknowledge your inescapable presence, witnessing forever against the finality of destruction, abandonment, and despair.

Litany

L: Look at our feet, Lord. Lives have been crushed to the ground, and we have trampled upon them. They have been spilt like water upon the ground, and we have stepped over them.

P: The Spirit sees, and hard the Spirit grieves; from side to side she rocks in torment.

L: Look at our eyes, Lord. Lives have been banished to the shadows, and we have looked away from them. They have stretched out their hands from the shadows, and we have brushed past them.

P: The Spirit sees, and hard the Spirit grieves; from side to side she rocks in torment.

L: Shall we lock our door upon the outcast?

P: Let us open the door *before* they knock, that the Spirit might find her consolation!

L: Shall we hammer our nail into their tree?

P: Let us tear down the cross *before* they plead, that the Spirit might rejoice.

L: When they hunger for bread, let us not throw them a stone,

P: But offer our bodies, that all might have life.

L: When they thirst for water, let us not pour out vinegar,

P: But offer ourselves, that all might have breath.

A: O Sorrow, where is your victory? O Grief, where is your sting?[53] For our feet are light on their missions of mercy, and our eyes are fast on the purposes of love.

Prayer for One Voice. O God, you know all things and are not

---

[53] Inspired by I Corinthians 15:55.

destroyed; you understand all things and are not desolate. For that which is destroyed you re-create, and that which is made desolate you restore.

How we envy you your strength, O God. And how we despair of our fragility! Often what we know condemns us, confuses us, conquers us. Often what we understand is so overwhelming that we run from it, so isolating that we abandon it, so incomplete that we surrender it. Intellect strives to govern the heart, and the heart rebels; the heart struggles to rule the intellect, and the intellect resists. Common sense contends with sentiment, they vie for control. Little do they realize that neither of them alone is sufficient.

O God, we are the Joabs of this day. Sometimes we are loyal to our emotions, but only until our hearts begin to break; then we become hard to guard them from harm, never minding the injury our hardness inflicts. Then, at other times, our reason reigns supreme, but often at the cost of being only half of who we are. Unable to link thought and feeling, practicality and personality, it is not long before we have murdered a wayward Absalom, against the command of love.

Make us *whole*, Lord, and we will be strong. Send to us, as to David, your messenger. Remind us through her that life is short, that death approaches, that there is no time for the outcast to remain outside us, for the exiled to remain beyond us, for the banished to remain against us. Your word will open the way between our head and our heart, that we might extend our hands without judgment *and* without folly. Your word will enable us to re-create what has been destroyed and to restore what has been made desolate. Yes, speak to us your word and, unlike Joab, we shall try to find a way to deal gently with Absalom—for your sake and for ours.

Benediction. Love one another, as Christ has loved us. Sacrifice for one another, as Christ has sacrificed for us. Forgive one another, as Christ has forgiven us. For we are not alone; we are members one of another—and members of the family of God.

Sunday Between August 14 and August 20 Inclusive

Lections: I Kings 2:10-12; 3:3-14; Psalm 111; Ephesians 5:15-20; John 6:51-58

Call to Worship
L: If you thirst for more than tears, come:
P: And the Lord our God shall give you drink.
L: If you hunger for more than ashes, come:
P: And the Lord our God shall give you bread.
A: Let us sip together the wine of the Kingdom, and the realm of God shall appear in our midst. Let us taste together the manna of heaven, and the reign of God shall fill the earth.

Invocation. O Lord, we invoke the power of life: to overcome strife, to endure suffering, to rise above affliction, and to pass beyond death. We ask that you bring us to peace, that you lead us to solace, that you restore us to happiness, and that you enter with us into eternity.

Litany
L: O God, this age in which we live! Two eyes look at the same world, and one regards it as beauty, and the other, as obscenity; one, as innocence, and the other, as sin.
P: Our vision is crossed, Lord. And still you desire that we walk in wisdom?
L: O God, this age in which we live! Two ears listen to the same world, and one hears it as praise, and the other, as slander; one, as truth, and the other, as fiction.
P: Our hearing is muddled, Lord. And still you desire that we walk in wisdom?
L: O God, this age in which we live! Two hands grip the same world, and one feels it as whole, and the other, as pieces; one, as ballast, and the other, as burden.
P: Our feelings are mixed, Lord. And still you desire that we walk in wisdom?
L: O God, if you would have us be wise, make clear our vision.

137

P: Heal us, Lord!

L: If you would have us be wise, sharpen our hearing.

P: Heal us, Lord!

L: If you would have us be wise, awaken our feeling.

P: Heal us, Lord!

A: Heal us, and then we shall take up our wisdom and walk!

Prayer for One Voice. O God, our feeble cry escapes our lips. Let it reach your ear!

We bear witness before you: upon earth, this is the day of distress. We have walked abroad, and where once we strolled through paradise, we tiptoe now on the edge of the abyss. Earth's life passes away like smoke, its bones burn like a furnace. Its heart is withered like dry grass. It forgets to eat all but ashes, it forgets to drink all but tears.

The body of this earth bears witness to the reality of death. We run to you with the message, we want to be of help; but we tremble. Have we the courage to confess that all is not well in Eden?

A battle rages, and life has been lost. We stand before David the king, the parent, our friend—and he asks us, "Is it well with Absalom?" And though we have witnessed a terrible scene, though we have pleaded to carry the news, though we have run fast and hard to arrive with the word before a simple stranger—now, in his presence, our courage falters. We lack the strength to label sin, to name misfortune, to grieve death. And so we stand aside, and the sorry message falls without sympathy from another's lips.

O God, our cry is feeble, but no cry can be so feeble that you do not hear. Incline your ear! Listen to us, that we might find the strength to heed the warnings we have heard. Do not hide your face! Look upon us, that we might find the courage to face the abominations we have seen.

For yours, O Lord, is this earth; yours, its creatures, and all that dwells therein. You are its ruler, and you love it greatly. And so, Creator, answer us speedily, answer us mightily; and in all haste and with all power we shall do your bidding, that all might deal gently with Absalom!

Benediction
L: Here in this place our thirst has been quenched.
P: Let us carry the cup beyond the door.
L: Here in this place our hunger has been sated.
P: Let us bear the bread into our world.
A: Let us carry the cup that it might be lifted; let us bear the bread that it might be broken. From life to life, God's life is given! From life to life, all life is saved!

Sunday Between August 21 and August 27 Inclusive

Lections: I Kings 8:1, 6, 10-11, 22-30, 41-43; Psalm 84; Ephesians 6:10-20; John 6:56-69

Call to Worship
L: Let us awaken from the deep night of the soul,
P: For God is dawning on the world like morning light,
A: Like the sun dancing forth on a cloudless morning.
L: Let us turn to the east with joy upon our lips,
A: May God's face shine upon us, and give us peace.[54]

Invocation. Your dawn breaks, O Lord. Send warm shafts of your spirit-light to fall upon our souls, frozen numb by the wintry winds of the night. Thaw the frost that has hardened upon us, which brings us death. And fill us with the fire of your spirit, which gives us life.

Litany
L: There is no God like you, O Lord—
M: In heaven above,
W: Or on earth beneath!
L: You keep covenant with those who walk in your ways,
M: And you seek covenant with all people—
W: All people from near and far—
L: That every creature on earth might know your name.
M: Therefore, let all people come together:

---

[54] See also Numbers 6:25-26.

139

W: To grow strong in your spirit,
L: And prepare to do battle;
M: To contend not against flesh and blood,
W: But against the forces of evil in high places.
L: O Lord, grant us your holy armor
M: That we might withstand the day of testing
W: And the night of trial,
L: And, having done all, to stand firm.
M: Let us pray in your Spirit,
W: Always remembering our love for one another
L: That we might boldly proclaim the gospel
M: In word as in deed,
W: In service as in spirit;
L: That we might continue to walk in your ways,
M: And tread this path with people from afar.
W: For you, O Lord, withhold no good thing—
L: No thing that is needed—
A: From those who walk uprightly, seeking your will!

Prayer for One Voice. O Lord, you unveil hidden things. You make clear misunderstood things. You revive forgotten things. You, O Lord, are the Great Revealer—the mysterious bard, the strange troubadour of love, the storyteller spinning wondrous tales of a great devotion, the poet composing a universe where the Creator romances creation.

You are the revealer of the eternal Word, but you do not reveal the Word to the world, once and for all time. Again and again it is sung and told and spun and lived. And while with each unveiling we behold something old and familiar, with each disclosure we also witness something new and peculiar. You fashion the Word to its age and its place. If it is to be sung, you wrap its tune around a contemporary beat. If it is to be told, you narrate the plot in a native tongue. If it is to be embodied, you sculpt its face in a fitting image.

Something old, something new—your revelation, O God, is at once eternal and momentary, at once complete and fragmentary. On it goes and forever it comes, as it always has gone, as it always shall come again.

But we, like your first disciples, are unprepared for your

revelation. We look for a savior: we want a new law, so long as it runs only so deep as the engravings on a stone tablet; we demand a new revelation, so long as it retains enough of the old that few changes are required. But this Jesus—his law cuts beneath tablets and appearances to life-blood; his revelation is fulfilled not only in life, but in death.

Like the disciples, we have little depth of understanding. We hear, and we say, "This is a hard saying; who can listen to it?" We murmur and argue and grumble and debate, for we cannot agree with one another, and this revelation does not agree with us. We want something simple, and this is an enigma. We want wisdom, and this seems folly. We want blessing, and this is sacrifice.

O Lord, help us to persevere. We fear that many of us will draw back, that we will refuse to go farther from the old truths and the old ways than we have already gone. Endow us with the courage of Peter, that we might confess that we are lost without you, that we have no truth without abiding in you, that we have no way without following you.

O Lord, send your Spirit! Open us to your singing and your speaking and your sending it *this* day; lest, in not seeing it today, we be blind to it tomorrow.

Benediction. Arm us, O God, with the sword of the Spirit, and put on us your armor, that we may be able not only to oppose evil but defeat it.

Sunday Between August 28 and September 3 Inclusive

Lections: Song of Solomon 2:8-13; Psalm 45:1-2, 6-9; James 1:17-27; Mark 7:1-8, 14-15, 21-23

Call to Worship
L: The Lord has dominion from sea to sea, from here to the ends of the earth.
P: A scepter of equity is in the Lord's hand,
L: As the Lord rides forth to defend the truth and to destroy all falsehood.

P: The hand of the Lord reaches out to lift up the needy and feed the hungry.

L: Therefore, with joy and gladness let us come into the presence of the Lord our God—

A: And praise the name of the Lord with the words of our lips and deeds of our lives!

Invocation. O God, we have come unto the hills, where earth and heaven meet. Whisper to us sweet things as the breeze stirs through blades of grass. Shout to us marvelous things as the river roars down its bed of stones. And in this center where the stillness of your whisper answers the thunder of your shout, let us find the fullness of your presence, wherein we find our help.

Litany

L: The way of the Lord is not easy. We must not cling to our own traditions, but prepare the day for God's transformations:

P: We must bear the light to those in darkness, and guide their feet into paths of peace.[55]

L: The way of the Lord is not easy. We must not offer our lipservice only, but withhold no measure of service in life:

P: We must make justice roll down like the waters, and righteousness like an ever-flowing stream.[56]

L: The way of the Lord is not easy. We must not act that others might notice, but fulfill the law that only God can see:

P: We must read the word placed in our minds, and obey the law written on our hearts.[57]

L: Let us hear, and let us understand.

P: Let us worship the Lord, not in name, but in truth; let us worship the Lord, not in vain, but with faith!

Prayer for One Voice. O God, your word of centuries ago reaches our ears, speaking in accents that are all too clear, of

---

[55] Inspired by Luke 1:79.
[56] Inspired by Amos 5:24.
[57] Inspired by Hebrews 8:10.

142

issues that are all too familiar, and of people we know all too well.

"Be doers of the word, and not hearers only, deceiving yourselves," James cries. Writing to first-century Christians, he might have been invoking the heroic image of Simon Peter—not the fisherman, but the disciple; not the slavish traditionalist, but the emancipated reformer. At his best, Peter was more than a follower of Jesus; he was your servant. At his best, he was quick to hear and slow to speak, honoring you with his heart as with his lips. At his best, he was not merely a hearer of your word; he was a doer of your word. At his best, Peter did not deny you, as he had thrice denied Jesus; he was prepared to die for you. At his best, Peter did die for you. So, too, according to tradition, did James and John and, after them, a whole host of martyrs and reformers through the centuries.

We *know*, O Lord, that faithfulness is no guarantor of reward. We *know* that righteousness is no bestower of blessings. We *know* that truth is no guardian against calamity. We *know* that love is no protector from hatred. We *know* that good does not always repay good; evil does not always find penalty. Yet how often we have thought, "We must be faithful; we can work ourselves through the gates of heaven." Thus, we have sometimes done your word with motives less than pure. Who among us would dare number ourselves among the sheep?[58]

The author of James knew full well the dangers in store for those who are quick not only to hear your word but to do it. Yet he boldly cried: "Do not be deceived! Be doers of the word, and not hearers only." Issued from the depths of a threatened church, yet dispatched from the heights of love, that cry took wing and flew through all of Christendom. O God, let it fly this day to us.

Benediction. O Lord, as you have called us together to be hearers of your word, send us forth to be doers of your word. As your word became flesh and dwelt among us, full of grace and truth, in Jesus of Nazareth, let it become flesh and dwell among our neighbors, full of grace and truth, in us.

---

[58] See Matthew 25:32-33.

Sunday Between September 4 and September 10 Inclusive

Lections: Proverbs 22:1-2, 8-9, 22-23; Psalm 125; James 2:1-17; Mark 7:24-37

Call to Worship
L: We are gathered to celebrate life's great gifts—
P: To worship the Lord who is the source of them all:
L: That the ears of us deaf may be opened—
P: To hear the words of truth and beauty;
L: That the tongues of us mute may be loosed—
P: To speak the words of love and duty.
A: The Lord seeks us. Come, let us seek the Lord.

Invocation. O Lord our God, you do nothing without declaring the good news through your servants. We thank you for the gift of language and for your willingness to engage us in dialogue. We thank you especially for your word made flesh in Jesus Christ—the word that clarifies all your other words. We pray that, in the quiet of this holy place and time, you will speak your clarifying word to us.

Litany
L: O God, who gives words the power to spread joy or sorrow, help us bridle our tongues.
P: Let our words give wings to our faith, supporting those in need of encouragement and challenging those in need of discipline.
L: When they who declare the easy lie to a friendly crowd turn to us,
P: Let us speak to them words of challenge.
L: When they who proclaim the hard truth to an angry crowd turn to us,
P: Let us speak to them words of support.
L: When people rail against the poor and disadvantaged,
P: Let us speak to them words of challenge.

144

L: When people speak up for the abused and oppressed,
P: Let us speak to them words of support.
L: When the champions of evil wax strong from vulgar popularity,
P: Let us speak to them words of challenge.
L: When the champions of good grow weary from social neglect,
P: Let us speak to them words of support.
L: O Lord, you have put into our mouths the power of death and life.
A: Help us, dear God, so to use this power as to spread life and not death.

Prayer for One Voice. O God, you endow us with gifts that go largely unused, you woo us with expectations that go largely unmet and you pursue us with offers that go largely unanswered. You astound us with your attention; apart from it, we would deem ourselves of little significance. Yet we dare not esteem lightly those whom you esteem highly, downgrade those whom you upgrade or expect little of those from whom you demand much. So, instead of debating our value, we choose simply to thank you. We thank you for your gracious gifts, your lofty expectations and your relentless offers—for loving us too deeply and too dearly to leave us alone.

If only we could say that, as you have loved us, so have we loved you. But we cannot. You instruct us with your testimonies, your statutes, your precepts, and your laws, but we ignore your teaching. Hearing, we hear not. You seek to enlighten us with your understanding, your insights, your words, and your wisdom, but we prefer the darkness to the light. Seeing, we see not. You challenge us with the commandments of your lawgivers and the oracles of your prophets, but we choose to be hearers rather than proclaimers of the word. Speaking, we speak not.

We live in a world that is often deaf, blind, and mute. For this we are deeply sorry, but we have helped to make it so. By our action and by our inaction, we have aggravated its afflictions. We have closed our ears to its harsh noises, shielded our eyes from its ugly sights, and remained tongue-tied before its vile deeds.

O Lord, take away not only our guilt but the indifference that allows us to remain as we are—and to like it. Create in us a clean heart and a right mind, so that, as the world's sounds grow loud, our hearing will grow sharp; so that, as the world's sights grow hideous, our seeing will grow percep- tive; and so that, as the world's mischief-makers grow powerful, our speaking will grow bold. Unstop our ears, O God, that we might hear the cries for justice. Open our eyes, that we might recognize the scars of oppression. And loose our tongues, that justice might find its voice and oppressors get their due.

Recalling the futility of pious words unaccompanied by righteous deeds, we pray for the wisdom to speak truly and the strength to act decisively. Let our deeds speak so loudly that the hearers of *our* words will become the doers of your *word.*

Benediction. O God, who has given us minds with which to discern your truth, hearts with which to discover your will and strength with which to fulfill your mission, we are grateful to you for these matchless gifts. Today, as we have gathered for worship, our minds have been awakened to your truth and our hearts to your will. Now, as we scatter for work, grant us the strength to perform your mission.

Sunday Between September 11 and September 17 Inclusive

Lections: Proverbs 1:20-33; Psalm 19; James 3:1-12; Mark 8:27-38

Call to Worship
L: In the beginning God said, "Let us create humanity in our own image." So God created humanity, male and female God created them.[59]

---

[59] See Genesis 1:1-27.

P: O come, let us praise the Lord our God: let us worship the Lord our Creator.

L: In the beginning was the Word, and all who received the Word were given power to become the children of God.[60]

P: O come, let us praise the Lord our God: let us worship the Lord our Redeemer.

L: Jesus said, "The Holy Spirit will teach you all things, and bring to your remembrance all that I have said."[61]

P: O come, let us praise the Lord our God: let us worship the Lord our Teacher.

A: O come, let us worship the Lord our God—our Creator, our Redeemer, and our Teacher.

Invocation. O God, in whom we behold not only the image of you but the likeness of ourselves, help us honestly to seek you. Deliver us from flippancy of tongue and fickleness of heart, that today's worship might prepare us for tomorrow's work. If today we are quick to endow you with gracious titles, make us equally quick tomorrow to honor you with gracious deeds.

Litany

L: The Holy Spirit, we were promised, will bring to our remembrance all that Jesus said and did.

P: Let us take seriously the faith for which he paid dearly.

L: When we report others' opinions of him, we are asked for ours;

P: Let us take seriously the faith for which he paid dearly.

L: After we hail him as the Christ, we rebuke him for expecting rejection;

P: Let us take seriously the faith for which he paid dearly.

L: When we gather for worship, we are warned against letting differences divide us;

P: Let us take seriously the faith for which he paid dearly.

---

[60] See John 1:1-12.
[61] See John 14:9-26.

L: When we begin to attract the privileged, we are reminded not to neglect the poor;

P: Let us take seriously the faith for which he paid dearly.

L: When we promise to follow him, we are counseled to take up our cross;

P: Let us take seriously the faith for which he paid dearly.

Prayer for One Voice. O God, whose name is above every name, we invoke your presence with mingled joy and hesitation: with joy, because we know that, before we turn in your direction, you have already turned in ours; yet with hesitation, because we also know that, as we have been quick to claim you as our heavenly parent, we have been slow to claim our neighbors as sisters and brothers. Despite our smallness, you have not withheld your name or your presence. Unwilling to accept the nay of yesterday as a nay for today, you pursue us with a grace and a patience beyond anything we deserve or understand. For this, O Lord, we adore you.

Face to face with your love, as undeniable as it is undeserved, we lament our failure to give it to others as freely as we receive it from you. Although we are unworthy of your love, we demand that others be worthy of ours. We define *worth* in terms not of your gospel but of our culture. We ignore the scriptural warning against showing partiality and bestow favor on those who earn what we earn, live as we live, vote as we vote, cater to the people to whom we cater, and shun the people whom we shun.

We act as if we would be content to be known by Jesus' name while mocking his values. As if his concern for the despised Samaritans held no significance, we continue to curse the enemies of our ancestors. As if his rebuke of the money-changers had no relevance, we continue to build our crystal cathedrals. As if his praise of peacemakers were of no consequence, we continue to worry more about the size of our arsenals than the supplies in our granaries. As if his warning against the bartering of our souls were of little moment, we continue to treat crossbearing as an option for those who cannot succeed in moneymaking.

For misunderstanding and misrepresenting you, O Lord, we ask your forgiveness. And we pray that here, as in Nazareth of Galilee, you will so open our eyes to the truth of Christ that we will understand him rightly and represent him faithfully.

Benediction. O God, whose name we have praised in the house of worship, make us equally quick to exalt your name in the world of work. As here we have honored you with the words of our mouths, let us there honor you with the deeds of our hands.

Sunday Between September 18 and September 24 Inclusive

Lections: Proverbs 31:10-31; Psalm 1; James 3:13–4:3, 7-8*a*; Mark 9:30-37

Call to Worship
L: The Lord sees the end from the beginning.
P: Wisdom begins with reverence for the Lord.
L: The Lord judges the immediate by the ultimate.
P: Wisdom begins with reverence for the Lord.
L: The Lord weighs the deed by the motive.
P: Wisdom begins with reverence for the Lord.
A: As we worship in your temple, we pray, O Lord, that you will bless us with a wisdom that the world can neither give nor take away.

Invocation. O God, you inspired Jesus to forsake the wisdom of the world for the folly of the cross. Prepare us to be disciples of such a Lord. Let us behold with him a world in which your will shall be done on earth as in heaven: a world in which we shall not only avoid, but destroy, temptation; a world in which we shall not only plead for, but practice, forgiveness. Anoint us, as you anointed him, to become the glad tidings we bear.

Litany
L: O Lord, your wisdom confounds the wise and exalts the foolish,

P: That we might sow the seeds of peace and reap the harvest of righteousness.

L: O Lord, your wisdom threatens the mighty and encourages the lowly,

P: That we might sow the seeds of peace and reap the harvest of righteousness.

L: O Lord, your wisdom puts down the strong and lifts up the weak,

P: That we might sow the seeds of peace and reap the harvest of righteousness.

L: O Lord, your wisdom dismisses the idle boast and embraces the humble deed,

P: That we might sow the seeds of peace and reap the harvest of righteousness.

A: Deliver us, O Lord, from the wisdom from below—the wisdom that is folly; that we might practice the wisdom from above—the folly that is wisdom.

Prayer for One Voice. Gracious God, the source of life and everything that increases its value, we adore you for all you are and all you do, not only for us but for all your children.

While grateful for all your gifts, we thank you, in particular, for the concerns that bind all humanity into a common family—the concerns through which you have turned the good earth into a global village and linked us together in a chain that, if broken, could spell ruin for us all. As we ponder these concerns, we are deeply troubled. At times, we second-guess you for saddling us so quickly with so great a responsibility. It is too heavy for us, demanding more strength than we possess and greater wisdom than we command. Yet we do thank you, O Lord. We thank you for having placed in us a trust to match our responsibility; for not abandoning us to *our* strength and *our* wisdom; and, for bestowing on our generation, as on no other, the rich legacy of human achievement.

We must confess, O Lord, that we have not done justice by this heritage. Not only have we disgraced some of its noblest values. We have left untouched vast stores of its traditions. Non-Christian religions have been dismissed with a wave of the hand. Economic systems different from our own have been treated with thinly veiled contempt. Customs preceding the industrial revolution have been described as uncivilized and their practitioners denounced as savages. This catalogue of shame could be greatly extended, but we will not aggravate our guilt by dwelling on it. Not that we seek a verdict of innocence on our past. We pray, rather, for the strength and courage and wisdom not to repeat it.

Open our hearts to the influence of your spirit, O God, that we might open our minds to the influence of other traditions. Help us respect the culture of others— its history, its religion, its education, its economy, its politics, its institutions—as we would have them respect ours; to approach it not with sympathy but with empathy; and not to speak *of* it without speaking *for* it.

We pray, O God, for the enlightenment and empowerment of all peoples. We pray for the grace to remove the cloud of self-righteousness with which we have obscured other races and nations. Help us raise their self-esteem by the respect with which we deal with them; to heighten their regard for justice, by the passion with which we contend for their rights; and to intensify their hatred of oppression, by our support for the oppressed. Let us so represent you to one another that you might reveal yourself in us all.

Benediction. Gracious God, in Jesus Christ you revealed the tyranny of earthly wisdom and the danger of heavenly wisdom. Send us forth, so transformed by our reverence for you, that we shall pursue the wisdom that is from above. Grant us not only the strength to resist the tyranny but the courage to risk the danger.

Sunday Between September 25 and October 1 Inclusive

Lections: Esther 7:1-6, 9-10; 9:20-22; Psalm 124; James 5:13-20; Mark 9:38-50

Call to Worship
L: All around the world people gather in the name of

Christ. Many of them believe as we do, yet they neglect the work for which we were anointed.   ·

P: They who are not for us are against us.[62]

L: All around the world people gather in the name of Christ. Some of them do not believe as we do, yet they do the work for which we were anointed.

P: They who are not against us are for us.[63]

A: We are called not to judge our neighbors but to witness to our God. O come, let us praise the Lord together!

Invocation. O God, who grants us the power to do mighty works but not the right to deny that power to others, we approach you in humility and confidence. We come before you confidently, for we have seen your likeness in Jesus Christ; yet we come humbly, because we have seen you not as you are, but only dimly, as in a mirror. So we do not pray for ecstatic visions—that our sight might be perfect and our understanding complete. We ask only that you be a lamp unto our feet and a guide for our journey.

Litany

L: O Lord, your fields are ready for the harvest, but the laborers are in short supply. We lament our role in driving them from your vineyard.

P: Search our hearts, O God, and lay bare our deceit.[64]

L: Let us remember those who wanted to do your work but were overwhelmed by our expectations.

P: Search our hearts, O God, and lay bare our deceit.

L: Let us remember those who were inspired by your spirit but were dismayed by our demands.

P: Search our hearts, O God, and lay bare our deceit.

L: Let us remember those who were committed to human dignity but were undercut by our suspicions.

P: Search our hearts, O God, and lay bare our deceit.

---

[62] See Matthew 12:30.
[63] See Mark 9:40.
[64] See Psalm 139:23.

L: O Lord, your fields are ready for the harvest, but the
    laborers are in short supply. We accept the task of
    drawing them to your vineyard.
P: Let us not confuse jealousy of self with jealousy for you.
L: When others make sacrifices in your name, let us trust
    their motives.
P: Let us not confuse jealousy of self with jealousy for you.
L: When others defer action in your name, let us respect
    their patience.
P: Let us not confuse jealousy of self with jealousy for you.
L: When others speak too loosely of you, let us forgive their
    rashness.
P: Let us not confuse jealousy of self with jealousy for you.
A: Help us, O Lord, so to live and love as to attract laborers
    to your vineyard.

Prayer for One Voice. Eternal God, in every age you have
entered into covenant, and in no age have you been without a
covenant people. We praise your holy name, not because you
have broken covenant with others to make covenant with us,
but because you have made your covenant to include us.

We are grateful, dear Lord, for fellow members of the
covenant—for all our co-workers in your service. Without
them, not only would your mission go unaccomplished, but
we could never enjoy the abundant life you promised. We
need one another. For without our mutual exchange—the
ongoing dialogue that enables us to learn from one another's
mistakes and to profit from one another's experience—we
would pose an even greater obstacle to your cause than we
do. We pray, therefore, that you will deepen our awareness
of and our appreciation for one another.

When we think of the ways we have impeded the work of
our co-laborers, we have enough guilt to go around. There is
much we should have done that we failed to do. And there is
much we did that we should not have done. We should have
accepted those by whose side we labored, but they could not
be true disciples of Christ, we seemed to feel, unless they
thought as we thought, felt as we felt, and acted as we acted.

O Lord, as we look to the future, we ask you to clean the

153

slate. Let us recall your teaching in Nazareth of Galilee: that it is more blessed to give than to receive; that we must lose our lives to save them; and that how we love is more important than what we believe. While you are no longer here to enflesh these words, your Spirit is not absent. Let it cease to be merely a presence of which we may take notice if we choose; make it a force with which we must come to terms.

O Christ, teach us to surround our jealousy for your name with respect and with reverence. Deliver us from the impulse to give ultimate answers to questions concerning immediate needs: when the sick come to us in need of medicine, the homeless in need of housing, the hungry in need of food or the jobless in need of work, grant us the wisdom to recognize that true evangelism puts humanity before religion, and the grace to acknowledge that true religion takes people more seriously than it takes itself.

Above all, O Lord, we pray for purity of heart—for the will to will one thing alone; for the will so to love that we will give ourselves for the world—the world for which you died.

Benediction. Gracious Lord, you have summoned us for a journey that will last a lifetime. Help us to foster the attitudes and cultivate the habits that will enable us to stay the course. Let us learn to do justice, love kindness and walk humbly with our God.[65]

Sunday Between October 2 and October 8 Inclusive

Lections: Job 1:1; 2:1-10; Psalm 26; Hebrews 1:1-4, 5-12; Mark 10:2-16

Call to Worship
L: Like children receiving a gift of love,
P: Like toddlers ripping open big mysteries from little packages,
A: Let us receive the presence of God.

---

[65] See Micah 6:8.

L: Let our pride in receiving be small,
P: And let our faith be great,
A: That we might plumb the depths of the grace God has given and cry no more tears over heights unattained.

Invocation. O God, who sanctifies and redeems us through one who has a common origin with ourselves, we celebrate our oneness with you. You declare that it is not good for us to be alone; and, behold, we are not alone. For though flesh perishes, though creatures tremble and all the world shakes, forever you abide. O God, who dwells in all and through all, reveal your fullness in our midst, that we might become fully yours.

Litany
L: Brothers and sisters, let us sing songs of praise and thanksgiving to our God,
P: For the Lord blots out the sins of our youth.
L: Let us proclaim aloud all the wondrous deeds of our God,
P: For the Lord guides us in the paths of righteousness.
L: Let us come and sit at the feet of our God.
P: For the Lord instructs us in the ways of truth and mercy.
L: Let us take refuge in the goodness of our God,
P: For the Lord sustains us in our pursuit of peace with justice.
L: Let us tell the world about the grace of our God,
P: For the Lord relieves our troubled hearts and brings us out of our distress.
L: Let us place our hand in the hand of our God,
P: For the Lord directs our feet away from discord and indifference.
L: Let us put our trust in no one but our God,
P: For only the Lord shows steadfast love and faithfulness.
L: Sisters and brothers, let us covet and cultivate the friendship of our God,
P: For the Lord keeps covenant with those who praise the name of the ruler of the universe.
A: O come, let us praise the Lord!

Prayer for One Voice. O God, how you test us! Even as the Pharisees and the disciples tested Jesus, you test us! You put to us the same choice that they put to him: shall we cling to our pride and seek to achieve our salvation? Or shall we trust your grace and dare to receive our salvation? Shall we accept your gift, or shall we reject it, thinking we must earn our due?

As if any human being could boast in your presence—the one by whose word the universe is designed! As if any laws that we might decree could be righteous in your presence—the one from whose mind true law is derived! As if any obedience to such laws could be perfect in your presence—the one by whose character perfection is defined!

We know, O God, that it is not obedience to rules that brings us to paradise. It is our ability to be grasped by your grace. Learn about grace, you have said, from the children. Learn from them about salvation. Their happiness depends not on strict rules but stable relationships. They learn more from forgiveness than from obedience. They receive as easily as they give—they can receive without earning and give without owing.

Better than we, children understand the oneness of the world, the give-and-receive of the world, the gifts and the givers of the world. By contrast, we have grown up: common sense prevails, old habits win out. We live by the law that you cannot get without giving. Somehow we must find the child within, and, holding its hand, we must save ourselves and our world. We must save ourselves and our world not only by moving within the freedom of your grace, but by abandoning the pride that will not let us budge.

Let us see our children, Lord! Let us see our children's children!

Benediction. Gracious God, as you have brought us together in this place in the name of Christ our Lord, through whom you created the world and shared with us a common origin, send us forth to express our oneness with him, the world, and one another. Let no one put asunder what you in Jesus Christ have joined together.

Sunday Between October 9 and October 15 Inclusive

Lections: Job 23:1-9, 16-17; Psalm 22:1-15; Hebrews 4:12-16; Mark 10:17-31

Call to Worship
L: Oh, that we knew where we could find the Lord!
P: Then we would lay our case before our God—
L: That we might learn how the Lord would answer us,
P: And hear what our God would say to us.
L: Will the Lord contend with us in the greatness of divine power?
A: No, our God will give heed to our cry!

Invocation. O God, in your sight a thousand years are a solitary yesterday. We would be consumed by such a vision of eternity, so hard and long have we stared at mortality. Yet you *would* consume us, desiring that we see the world as you do. How hard it is to enter your kingdom!

Look upon us with love, Lord; we dream of this heavenly treasure, all the while keeping one eye on our earthly possessions. Send your word to strike softly our eyes and to pierce sharply our hearts, lest we be dismayed at the sight of you, and go away sorrowful.

Litany
L: Man, why do you not seek me? Woman, why do you not draw near?
P: But we do seek you, Lord. We go forward, but you are not there; we go backward, but we cannot perceive you. If only we could lay our case before you!
L: You say that you have sought me. How have you sought me?
P: We have held fast to your steps; we have kept your way and not turned aside. Yet our integrity is hid from your sight.
L: Before my word no creature is hidden. All are opened, laid bare to my eyes.

157

P: From our youth we had thought ourselves good. But now we are hemmed in by the night; a thick darkness enshrouds our lives.

L: And now you groan with all of creation, awaiting in hope your day of salvation.[66]

P: From our youth we had thought our works could save us.

L: But now you hope for what you do not see; now you rest on what you cannot do.[67]

P: From our youth we had thought: with us all things are possible.

L: But now you know that in all things you are more than conquerors only through my love.[68]

P: If you be for us, who can be against us? Let us come before you with thanksgiving, for now we are sure that neither death nor life, nor angels, nor principalities, nor things present, nor things to come, nor powers, nor height, nor depth, nor anything else in all creation, will be able to separate us from your love.[69]

Prayer for One Voice. O God, how hard it is to enter your Kingdom! Its gates open among us, but they are not easy to spy. Its heralds sit among us, but they are not easy to spot. We rely on what we see and overlook the mysteries of the unseen. We depend on what we hear and neglect the secrets of the silent.

Your revelation offers us clues in our search, Lord, but they often seem contradictory. In one breath you whisper, "Become like children!" In the next you confide, "You must move beyond your youth!"

You told our parents, "You shall love the Lord your God with all your heart, and with all your soul, and with all your might. And these words which I command you this day shall be upon your heart; and you shall teach them diligently to

---

[66] Inspired by Romans 8:22-23.
[67] Inspired by Romans 8:24-25.
[68] See Romans 8:37.
[69] See Romans 8:31*b*, 38-39.

your children.''[70] And yet you have told us, "Leave your parents and your homes, and follow me."

We have much to learn, O God. In childhood, in innocence, without deep understanding of good and evil, standing only on the foundation of right and wrong that our parents have laid: here we learn about obedience and self-discipline. But you would have us grow in spirit as we grow in body. Therefore, in age, in maturity, our understandings of the good and evil that lay without *and* within us must deepen. And, as they deepen, they will seek a foundation firmer than the rules of childhood. For what child can believe that good behavior will not be rewarded, that bad behavior will not be punished? Yet *we* know that the rain falls upon the good and the evil alike. And what child can count the cost of discipleship? Yet many of *us* have walked away from you in dismay, unable to surrender into your hands what we esteem most highly.

In childhood we learn much about obedience, O God. But those of us who learn its lessons best will one day have all the more to learn about forgiveness and grace. The greater our confidence in our obedience, the greater our danger of pride. The greater our awareness of our own righteousness, the dimmer our awareness of sin. The greater our allegiance to our own laws, O God, the weaker our adherence to your will.

Help us grow up, Lord. We would leave everything and follow you, but we are feeble. The best of what we have, the greatest of what we believe ourselves to be—we have reckoned it as your blessing upon our faithfulness. But we are no longer children. Look upon us with love and remind us, "No one is good but God alone." Look upon us with love, and challenge us, "If your spirit is strong, give *all* that you have, and follow me."

Look upon us with mercy, O Lord, not with judgment; and inspire in us the strength to step beyond the world of law to the world of love, where faithful existence is not for our own gain but for your glory.

---

[70] See Deuteronomy 6:5-7.

Benediction. O God, as here we have enthroned you on our praises, let us go forth to enthrone you in our hearts. But let us not walk alone. Go with us, dear Lord, that we may grow vulnerable in our sin, strong in your forgiveness, and faithful in our obedience, now and forever.

Sunday Between October 16 and October 22 Inclusive

Lections: Job 38:1-7, 34-41; Psalm 104:1-9, 24, 35c; Hebrews 5:1-10; Mark 10:35-45

Call to Worship
L: Servants of God, lift up your heads—
P: That the Lord of life may behold our eyes!
L: Servants of God, lift up your hands—
P: That the Lord of life may bless our works!
L: Servants of God, lift up your hearts—
P: That the Lord of life may abide within!
A: The Lord of life will abide within!

Invocation. O Teacher, we dare not make demands of you. Unlike James and John, we do not claim the honor of sitting beside you in glory. We ask only that you make our hearts the seat of your presence, that we might serve your purpose as zealously as we have served our own.

Litany
L: My disciples do not ask to be seated on either my right hand or my left.
P: They ask only that they be able to drink the cup that I drank, and to be baptized with the baptism with which I was baptized.
L: They do no violence,
P: But their enemies cannot endure their peace.
L: They speak no lie,
P: But their enemies cannot abide their truth.
L: They shun no neighbor,
P: But their enemies cannot tolerate their love.
L: They abandon no hope,

P: But their enemies cannot bear their faith.

L: I have seen their anguish, and I will not be silent. But where are *you*, my mighty throng? Do you sit together and wink at hate?

P: Wrap us in shame if we slander your disciples with silence!

L: Do you plot revenge in secret? Do you gild your anger with harmless words?

P: Clothe us in disgrace if we betray your disciples with a kiss!

L: Then be not far from them! Bestir yourselves, and awaken to their cause! Deliver them according to my will! Do not let their enemies rejoice in their destruction!

Prayer for One Voice. O God, who shows us how to serve through the service of Jesus Christ, look upon us with understanding. We have dedicated ourselves to the service of folly; and finally, in the noontide of our foolishness, we have the gall to ask with the sons of Zebedee, "Teacher, we want you to do for us *whatever we ask of you.*"

In the high noon of your infinite mercy, you ask, "What do you want me to do for you?" Unrepentant, we muster the further audacity not to ask, but to *demand*, "Grant us to sit beside you in your glory." When you gently warn that we do not know what we are asking, we are impudent enough to claim, "We are able to drink the cup that you drink, and to be baptized with the baptism with which you are baptized." You are right, Lord; we do not know what we ask, for the cup is filled with the wine of servanthood, and the baptism is unto sacrifice—even to the point of suffering. And that service, that sacrifice, *is* your glory.

We do not understand, but you do. And so, you are patient. You tolerate our prideful indiscretions, our arrogant presumptions. And then, you take up your teaching again, for it is plain that we do not yet understand what greatness resides in the choice to be servant, what majesty abides in the choice to be least.

Forgive our slow learning, God. Forgive our blustery confidence that erupts in speech when silence would be better, yet holds its tongue when one word could be decisive. And forgive our haughty swaggering, that struts amidst the weak when kneeling would be better, yet bends the knee when one step could be forever.

We ask your forgiveness, O Lord, in the name of the One who came not to be served but to serve. We ask forgiveness, that by your great mercy we might find that we *are* able, despite and because of who we are.

Benediction. Go to the world in confidence, for there the table of the Lord is spread. Draw near; drink from its cup, and receive the mercy of God. Draw near; partake of its bread and find the grace of God. Go, and the feast shall be to you as you shall be to your neighbor: a very present help in time of trouble.

Sunday Between October 23 and October 29 Inclusive

Lections: Job 42:1-6, 10-17; Psalm 34:1-8, 19-22; Hebrews 7:23-28; Mark 10:46-52

Call to Worship
L: O come, let us magnify the Lord,
P: That the afflicted might hear and be glad!
L: Let our souls boast in the Lord,
P: That the lame might leap for joy!
L: Let our tongues proclaim the glory of the Lord,
A: That the fearful might taste, and see that the Lord is good!

Invocation. O God, by the waters of our exile, we sit and weep, remembering our home. How can we sing your song in a foreign land?[71]

We are estranged from ourselves, we are alienated from one another. O God, you know our weakness: have compassion upon us; send your Spirit to heal us and to prepare the way for our return. Lead us by the still waters,

---

[71] Inspired by Psalm 137:1, 4.

restore our souls.[72] And your praise shall always be on our lips, and we shall exalt your name together.

Litany

L: O Lord, we are like blind Bartimaeus, but we are not bound by our affliction;

P: We are not chasing a wild fantasy, but dwelling amidst our heart's desire.

L: Yesterday we were defeated;

P: Today we are triumphant.

L: Yesterday we sighed in sorrow;

P: Today we shout for joy.

L: Yesterday we wept in grief;

P: Today we weep in gratitude.

L: Yesterday we doubted you;

P: Today you lead us home.

L: Yesterday our step was a hesitant stagger;

P: Today our step is a firm stride.

L: Yesterday we had met our end;

P: Today we have begun again.

L: O Lord, we *are* like blind Bartimaeus,

P: We *have* received our heart's desire.

A: For you have visited our despair, and we have embraced our joy. It is you whom we have sought; it is we whom you have found!

Prayer for One Voice. O Christ, you are our great interceder! Even as mighty forces in our world conspire to tear us apart, your powerful spirit schemes to reconcile us. You are the herald of this, your homecoming—the bringing in of the blind, the opening up of the closed-minded, the softening up of the hardhearted, the lifting up of the downtrodden. And the reunion continues to this day—in this life and the next.

We confess our need for reunion, Lord. And we concede that we stand with a foot on either side of the fence. On the one side, we number ourselves among the blind and the

[72] See Psalm 23:2b-3.

163

downtrodden, among the exiled and the excluded. In different ways each of us has known the pain of being shut out. The isolation, the frustration, the exasperation of being told and shown that we do not belong, that we are not wanted—it has frozen into a hard core in the center of our existence, and soon we have become too afraid to care anymore, to share anymore.

On the other side, we number ourselves among the close-minded and the hardhearted, among those who banish and bar. In different ways each of us has shut someone out. By word and deed we have isolated, frustrated, and exasperated our neighbors, letting them know that they do not belong, that they are not wanted. Our cruelty has hardened into a cold stone in the center of our existence, and soon we have become too blind to care anymore, to share anymore.

Yes, we confess our need for reunion, Lord. But before we can reunite with others, we must reunite our different selves. That within us which we guard must be relinquished; that which we deny must be owned. We must come home from our inner exile before we can return from the outer.

Heal our sight that we might behold ourselves clearly. If we have long been blinded by fantasies of our own greatness, as were James and John, open our eyes to our arrogance. If we have long been blinded by fears of our own flaws, as was Bartimaeus, reveal to us our timidity. Do not rebuke us for asking for vision, as your disciples rebuked the pleading beggar, but grant us the greatness that comes with humility and the courage that overcomes weakness.

Heal our sight, O Lord, and we shall declare: We have heard of you by the hearing of the ears, but now our eyes see you. And we shall praise your name, saying: You have heard our cry, and delivered us from all our fears!

Benediction. We were blind beggars sitting by the roadside. As people approached, they would pass quietly by on the other side. But at the approach of the Lord, we cried out; we sprang up and begged for our sight. We have not been rebuked. So let us go now, serving in the spirit of the one who serves without pause and seeing in the spirit of the one who sees without scorn.

Sunday Between October 30 and November 5 Inclusive

Lections: Ruth 1:1-18; Psalm 146; Hebrews 9:11-14; Mark 12:28-34

Call to Worship
L: The Lord our God is *one* God:
P: Let us rejoice with all our heart, for the joy of the Lord shall never be spent!
L: The Lord our God is *one* God:
P: Let us exult with all our soul, for the spirit of the Lord shall never be broken!
L: The Lord our God is *one* God:
P: Let us give thanks with all our mind, for the will of the Lord shall never be foiled!
L: The Lord our God is *one* God:
P: Let us strive with all our strength, for the power of the Lord shall never be thwarted!

Invocation. O God, whether we call you Father or Mother, Guardian or Friend, you soar above all names to that name which is unutterable. Whether we think of you as judgmental or gentle, unapproachable or accessible, you transcend all thoughts to that thought which is unthinkable. O God, you are more than we can say; speak to us. O God, you are more than we can comprehend; embrace us. For you are the one God, and we are your people.

Litany
L: Teach us, O Lord, the will of our God,
P: And we will interpret it for the world.
L: Whisper to us the demands of our Sovereign;
P: Our hearts will proclaim them from the housetops.[73]
L: Turn us from our frenzied pursuit of trivia;

---

[73] See Luke 12:3.

P: Our souls will take up the quest for meaning.
L: Lead us in the paths of your righteousness;
P: Our minds will delight in explaining them.
L: Confirm our resolve to unveil the secrets of your heart;
P: Our strength will persist in removing your masks.
L: Yes, teach us, O God, the mysteries of your ways,
P: For nothing is hidden but to be made plain; nothing made secret, but to be brought to light.[74]
L: And yet all prophecies shall pass away,
P: And all mysteries and knowledge be incomplete—
A: Unless perfect love be moving among us—bearing all things, believing all things, hoping all things, enduring all things.

Prayer for One Voice. Creator God, incline your ear to our hearts, for they long for you. Send your song to our souls, for they wait for you. Whisper your mysteries to our minds, for they search for you. Match your purposes to our strengths, for they rest in you. O God who hears and serenades us, who inspires and moves us, hear our prayer!

Creator-God, you fashion us from the earth. Made of the dust, we are tossed about by the wind; we are scattered around and trampled underfoot. Then, when all is done, we return to the dust from which we come. Such is the clay of which we are made.

And yet, you breathe *your* breath into our nostrils. Quickened by your spirit, we command the winds; we rise above the storm and utter, "Be still!" And, when all is done, we return to the spirit from which we come. Such is the soul of which we are formed.

What cryptic creatures we are, such a mix of this world and the next! And yet *we* are the ones who presume to ask the questions of *you;* we are the ones who dare to doubt. We are the skeptics and the cynics trying to trap you in our snares of reason and rebellion.

Are we really different from the chief priests and the

---

[74] See Mark 4:22.

166

elders, whose anxiety about human authority exceeded their respect for your authority?[75] Are we really different from the Pharisees and the Herodians, whose worry about Caesar transcended their worship of you? Are we really different from the Sadducees, whose concern about the future life dwarfed their interest in the present life?

No, Lord, we are not so different. The chief priest rules, the elder advises, the Pharisees and Herodians and Sadducees argue within us from morning till night. We walk out of the door at dawn, and we must decide until dusk, "What is right? What is correct? What is best? What is *just?*"

O God, give us more than wisdom. Grant us the understanding of the scribe, who put a question to Jesus not in suspicion but in faith. Let us ask, with him, "Which commandment *is* the first of all?" And when you answer, "Love me, and love *them,*" opening your arms wide to the world, let us find the courage to say, "You are right, Teacher!" And even though you have given us more than we requested—not one commandment but two, not twice as hard but ninety-times-nine—let us exclaim, "Yes! You *are* right!" Even though you express not ceremonial but *personal* concerns, let us vow, "Yes—to love you and to love one's neighbor as oneself, it *is* much more than all offerings and sacrifices!"

To gain this understanding, to walk in this path—this is the purpose for which you have made us. From the dust of the earth and the breath of heaven, you have fashioned us not in the image of the chief priests or the elders, but in *your* image—and in the image of this scribe, who was not far from your kingdom.

Benediction. Hear, O people! The Lord has written the commandment of love on our hearts. Let us go forth to write its message on the heart of the world.

---

[75] References in this paragraph are to the three tests put to Jesus by these groups just prior to the scribe's question in Mark 12:28.

Sunday Between November 6 and November 12 Inclusive

Lections: Ruth 3:1-5; 4:13-17; Psalm 127; Hebrews 9:24-28; Mark 12:38-44

Call to Worship
L: Heaven walks upon the earth! Where once was only a cup of meal,
P: A loaf is broken, and hunger is filled.
L: Heaven walks upon the earth! Where once was only a drop of water,
P: A chalice is lifted, and thirst is slaked.
L: Let us praise the Lord as long as we live;
P: Let us praise our God while we have being—
A: For our last two coins shall make a treasure and our poverty of spirit shall become God's wealth!

Invocation. O God, long have we put our trust in rulers, in mere mortals. But when breath departs, they return to the earth. Their answers, however timely, are not timeless.

But your purpose, Lord, endures forever. It is you who keeps faith with us. And to you we cry! Execute your justice for the oppressed and give your food to the hungry; set the captive free and lift up the downtrodden; watch over the lonely and uphold the abandoned—until we find our strength, in you and in one another.

Litany
L: Ruth begged Naomi, her mother-in-law, to take her back to Bethlehem.
P: And the lonely widow took her daughter-in-law to her home.
L: Naomi was deeply grieved that she had so little food to offer Ruth.
P: But she had a relative who was a man of wealth, and she sent Ruth to him.
L: Boaz allowed Ruth to gather grain among the sheaves after the reapers.

P: Then, giving her six measures of barley, he said to her, "You must not return to your mother-in-law empty-handed."

A: O, the last shall be first, and the first shall be last, here in the kingdom of God!

L: Jesus the prophet cried out for truth,

P: But he heard tedious prayers.

L: Jesus the prophet sought signs of great faith,

P: But he witnessed only a parade of gestures.

L: So Jesus the prophet warned the people, "Beware of those who guard their threshing floor and hoard their measures of barley; who feast on their abundance, then refuse even the gleanings to the poor!"

P: But then a poor widow approached in quiet and did what no other had done. She gave her last penny for a stranger in need, withholding no coin for herself. Yet her little wealth was never spent, and her life was not consumed!

A: Oh, the last shall be first, and the first shall be last, here in the kingdom of God!

Prayer for One Voice. O God, hear our prayer! For the story of the widow commended by Jesus has convicted us! It has shined upon the shadowy reaches of our souls, bringing to light our hunger for glory and our passion for power; our secret longing to stand out in and above the crowd; our terrible need to prove ourselves worthy before the world by appearing to be worthy before you.

We gather weekly to worship you, to give you praise and offerings, but this day you greet us with a shattering word:

"Who requires of you this trampling in my courts?" you thunder. "Bring no more vain offerings. I cannot endure iniquity and solemn assembly. Your feasts, my soul hates; they have become a burden to me, I am weary of bearing them. When you spread forth your hands, I will hide my eyes from you; even though you make many prayers, I will not listen.

"Wash yourselves! Make yourselves clean; cease to do evil, learn to do good; seek justice, correct oppression; *defend the orphan, plead for the widow,*" you cry.[76]

---

[76] See Isaiah 1:12-17.

169

This is what you require, Lord. Your voice drowns our every sermon and prayer and song with the reminder, "Let there be no joy without justice, no rejoicing without righteousness!"

Woe to us, O God, for we have not done what we have preached, we have not meant what we have prayed![77] We have cleaned the outside of the cup without first cleaning the inside; we are like whitewashed tombs filled with dead bones.

Woe to us, for we have laid heavy burdens on other shoulders while refusing to touch them with our own hands!

Woe to us, for we have sought places of honor while leaving others in places of harm!

Woe to us, for we have built shrines for yesterday's prophets and monuments for yesterday's saints, while crucifying the prophets and stoning the saints of today!

Woe to us, for we have traversed land and sea to make a single convert, only to make that convert twice as much a child of misery as ourselves!

Woe to us, for we have stood outside the gates of your Kingdom to bar another from entering!

Woe to us, for we have tithed sweetly, offering up herbs and spices, while neglecting the weightier matters of justice and mercy and faith!

O God of the forsaken, we deem ourselves virtuous, but the example of the widow has declared us villains. While we have stood off at a distance, Jesus has commended the widow of Jerusalem for taking a leap of faith; for offering up all she possesses at the risk of her life, putting to shame those who tithe out of their abundance. While we have stood off at a distance, Jesus has watched her give away her last coin; at the risk of her own welfare, she has surrendered all she has for the welfare of others.

O God, what sacrifices she has made with her life while we have tithed in the temple! Those two copper coins—so insignificant in themselves, gifts smaller than the smallest, yet greater than the greatest!

---

[77] The following lines are based on Matthew 23.

We have sinned, Lord, and we scatter from you, having seen the truth of what we do and who we are. Gather us gently together again, as a hen gathers her brood under her wings, and we shall come in! For this day we shout with one voice, "Blessed are the prophets! Blessed are the widows! Blessed are they who come in the name of the Lord!"

Benediction. Let us go and make our contribution to God, to this world and all who dwell therein. Let us not scramble to sit in the most honorable places or rush to recite the longest prayers. But let us, in our giving, offer up all the living we have.

Sunday Between November 13 and November 19 Inclusive

Lections: I Samuel 1:4-20; I Samuel 2:1-10; Hebrews 10:11-18, 19-25; Mark 13:1-8

Call to Worship
L: I saw a great vision in the night; I saw a new world coming, for the first had passed away.[78]
P: We heard a great voice in the night; we heard the Lord saying, "Be not alarmed. The end is not yet."
L: There is no rock like our God. The Lord gives courage to the faithful!
A: The Lord reigns; let us rejoice and be glad!

Invocation. Our world is in eclipse, Lord. The sun has been blotted out, the moon sheds no light, the stars are dropping from the skies—all is night. We have even lost faith in our laws; now we must trust the law you write upon the heart.
   O God, we sit in darkness; let us see a great light![79]

Litany
L: The time approaches when the lightning of forgiveness shall flash forth through all clouds of condemnation.

---

[78] Inspired by Revelation 21:1-6.
[79] See Isaiah 9:2.

171

P: Of that day not an angel knows.

L: The time approaches when the knife of mercy shall lay bare all thoughts of vengeance.

P: Of that hour not a mortal sees.

L: The time is coming when the robe of grace shall replace all trappings of pride.

P: Of that hour not an angel knows.

L: The time is coming when the eyes of compassion shall pierce the masks of prejudice.

P: Of that day not a mortal sees.

L: The time draws near when the heart of love shall conquer all arms of force.

P: Of that hour not an angel knows.

L: The time draws near when the vigil of faith shall dispel all phantoms of fear.

P: Of that day not a mortal sees.

L: The day approaches, the day is coming, the day draws near that no angel knows!

P: O God, let *this* be the day!

L: The hour approaches, the hour is coming, the hour draws near that no mortal sees!

P: O God, let *this* be the hour!

Prayer for One Voice. O God, we give thanks to you! We proclaim the glory of your Kingdom! We tell of your power! We declare to all the world your mighty deeds and glorious splendor!

We bless your name, Lord, for by your grace are we saved; by your mercy, forgiven; by your forbearance, accepted; by your love, restored! And by this grace are we made gracious; and by this mercy, merciful; and by this forbearance, forebearing; and by this love, loving!

This is so—not because of anything we have done, but because of what *you* have done! As the author of Hebrews declared, "Every priest stands daily at services, offering repeatedly the same sacrifices, which can never take away sins." But Jesus Christ, once and for all, embodied our relationship with you. And the Holy Spirit works at all times to write its good news upon our hearts. Yes, our salvation is

172

already accomplished, not by our acts, but by your act—not in another world, but in this world; not in another time, but in this time. All this you have promised.

And still more. For in your boundless love, you have vowed, "I will remember your sins and misdeeds no more." All is done, all is forgiven—even before our wavering, even before our failing, even before our pleading, even before our trembling. How can we not bless your name!

Yours is a name terrible in its mystery. We do not know what visage lies behind it. Hannah saw you as the One who set the world on the pillars of the earth, and as the One who brings low the mighty and lifts high the meek. Isaiah conceived you as "Mother"; he uttered your word to Israel, "Can a woman forget her sucking child, that she should have no compassion on the child of her womb? I will not forget you!"[80] And Jesus regarded you as "Father"; he told of your provision even for the birds of the air and the lilies of the field.[81]

Who are you, O God, who remembers your creatures, but no more their sin? You are everything and no-thing. You are the terrifying door into the unknown and the comforting embrace at the threshold!

O Lord, we call upon your name, which is above every name and gives meaning to all names. Usher us through that door, and we shall serve you, whose realm is eternal and whose dominion is everlasting!

Benediction. Look upon sin with compassion, and you shall see mercy. Look upon oppression with compassion, and you shall see justice. Look upon time with love, and you shall enter eternity. Look upon space with love, and you shall enter glory.

Christ the King
Last Sunday After Pentecost

Lections: II Samuel 23:1-7; Psalm 132:1-18; Revelation 1:4b-8; John 18:33-37

---

[80] Inspired by Isaiah 49:15.
[81] See Matthew 6:25 f.

Call to Worship

L: The days are coming when people shall stop saying, "As the Lord lives who brought Israel out of Egypt . . . ,"

P: And turn their attention away from what God *did* to what God *is doing*.

L: The days are coming when people shall stop saying, "As the Lord lives who brought the church out of bondage . . . ,"

P: And turn their attention away from what God *did* to what God *is doing*.

A: The Lord is present here and now! Let us rise up to meet and praise our God.

Invocation. Gracious God, who rules over all rulers but in a manner unlike any of them, we celebrate the promise fulfilled in Jesus Christ. When we compare their rule with his, we can only marvel at the difference. Their rule scatters their subjects; his, gathers them. Their rule breeds fear; his, hope. We prefer his rule to theirs, yet we permit theirs to eclipse his. So we pray, O God, that you will grant us the wisdom and courage so to enthrone your will that Christ, if he cannot rule through our leaders, will at least rule over us.

Litany

L: I am Christ, the pioneer and perfecter of your faith;

P: The beginning and the end.

L: The atom and the universe;

P: The one and the many.

L: The birth and the death;

P: The rise and the fall.

L: The dawn and the dusk;

P: The spring and the winter.

L: The rain and the rainbow;

P: The seed and the harvest.

L: The quest and the return;

P: The dream and the remembrance.

L: The foundation and the spire;

P: The promise and the fulfillment.

L: The baptism and the requiem;

P: The silence and the word.
A: I am the Alpha and the Omega, who is and was and is to come: Life, forevermore!

Prayer for One Voice. Eternal God, who was and is and is yet to be, we bow before you in awe and adoration. When life pushes us into a corner, we run from you only to find that from you there is no escape—that, no matter how we get off the course, you will not let us off the hook. For this, dear Lord, we are grateful. How good it is to know that we are loved by anybody. Yet how much better it is to know that the One who loves us, above all others, is the God of creation and the Lord of history—the Savior of the world and the ruler of the universe.

For centuries we have hailed you as our God and called ourselves your people. We have worshiped you as King of kings and called all other monarchs your agents. Yet we have not judged their rule by yours, measured their law by yours or tested their teaching by yours. Confronted by your demand for a clear-cut either/or, we have opted for Caesar's offer of a both/and. Face to face with Caesar's agents, we have taken the path of least resistance. When they weighted the scales of justice on the side of the strong, we were not blind, yet we remained silent. When they raised the costs of education beyond the reach of the masses, we recognized the inequity, yet we remained silent. When they inflated the price of political office in favor of the rich, we saw the danger, yet we remained silent. If only we could plead ignorance!

But we were not ignorant—only silent. We had already begun to see the handwriting on the wall. We knew even then that the cost of our compromise would run high and one day compromise your rule. Now that the day for payment is at hand, we will not insult you by pleading either ignorance or innocence, for we are as guilty as sin. We were aware, O Lord, that your dominion is not of this world. Yet we have behaved as if it were. We betrayed you, but you were not the only victim. There were others, many others: not only those who looked to us for guidance, but those whom we might have led to look to you.

175

Grant us, O Lord, the courage to put our sin behind us even as you have put it behind you. Help us, henceforth, so to live as to bear witness to the truth for which Christ lived and died and still lives. Guide us by your spirit that our neighbors, when they turn to us, will find clarity in the midst of confusion; support, in the midst of sorrow; unity, in the midst of division; purpose, in the midst of aimlessness; and you, in the midst of despair. So fill us with your love that we might become temporal witnesses to your eternal rule. Let us hope that, as a consequence, the rulers of this world will accept your rule—a rule that is not of this world.

Benediction. O Christ, you reign over the rulers of the earth. Yet your rule is not of this world. As you send us forth, help us remember that the domain of your rule is not a particular land but the human heart; that the method of your rule is not the demand from above but the choice from below; and that the symbol of your rule is not a crown but a cross.

Celebration of Special Occasions

New Year's Eve/Day

Lections: Ecclesiastes 3:1-13; Psalm 8; Revelation 21:1-6*a*;
Matthew 25:31-46

Call to Worship
L: As infants you chanted the glory of God;
P: As babes we sang to the heavens!
L: Now, sing to the Lord a new song!
    Let your fingers play skillfully upon the strings—[82]
P: For the heavens are the work of *God's* fingers!
    The moon and the stars they hung in the sky!
A: How majestic is the Lord in all the earth!
    How majestic is God's name!

Invocation. O Creator, you have made us little less than
yourself; you have crowned us with glory and honor. We are
altogether too mindful of this. Having tasted a drop of glory,
we have become drunk; having climbed to the height of
honor, we have become faint.

 We have been altogether too mindful of *our* divinity, and
too little mindful of *yours.* Who *are* we that you are mindful of
us, that you should care for us, sobering us up when we are
drunk on glory and lifting us up when we have fallen from
honor? We do not know the answer, O God; we only trust
that you *will* answer, this day and always.

Litany
L: For everything there is a season,
P: And a time for every matter under heaven.
L: Therefore, if this is a time to be born, let us emerge from
    the womb with a cry;

---

[82] See Psalm 33:3.

P: If this is a time to die, let us say farewell with a smile.

L: If this is a time to plant, let us scatter the seed with a prayer;

P: If this is a time to harvest, let us reap the grain with a song.

L: If this is a time to break down, let us topple the walls with a shout;[83]

P: If this is a time to build up, let us raise the foundation with care.[84]

L: If this is a time to mourn, let us catch the tears with a chalice;

P: If this is a time to dance, let us leap the moon with a laugh.

L: If this is a time to embrace, let us wrap the world with a ribbon;

P: If this is a time to stand alone, let us face the crowd with a mirror.

L: If this is a time to remain silent, let us proclaim the truth with a deed;

P: If this is a time to speak, let us counsel the words with the heart.

L: If this is a time to do battle, let us sustain the weak with a vision;

P: If this is a time to make peace, let us anoint the wounds with a balm.

L: For everything there is a season,

P: And a time for every matter under heaven;

A: O Lord, teach us to know the times!

Prayer for One Voice. O God, you have made everything beautiful in its time. The beasts of the field, the birds of the air, the fish of the sea—these are the works of your hands, yet they are part of a much greater work. They are but a few of the tiny stitches in a beautiful garment, a robe of many colors sewn together by your needle and worn by your universe. Eternally old, it sometimes shows its wear. Eternally new,

---

[83] Inspired by Joshua 6:20.
[84] Inspired by I Corinthians 3:10 f.

you gather it up in your lap for mending. You are careful not to use too fresh a patch, for, if it is too new, it will tear away from the garment, and a worse rip will be made. But the patch *will* be new, just the same, and the garment will be the stronger for it.

We, too, are the works of your hands, O God. And we are different from the beasts and the birds and the fish, for you have made us to know and to question, to think and to reflect: upon ourselves, one another and you. You have set us in history, in *time*—to be born, to eat and drink and take pleasure in our toil, to die. But you have also sent eternity into our midst—to show us how to be *re*born. You have sent Christ to tell us not to keep looking over our shoulder, but to be looking toward the horizon; not to idolize what used to be, but to prepare for what is going to be; not to glory in the stories of what happened then, but to proclaim the good news of what is happening *now*.

This is our new year, Lord. You have given us this time to recapture a glimpse of the eternity that moves and breathes among *us*. For whatever reason you are mindful of us, for whatever reason you care for us, for whatever reason you equip us to uncover the treasures of wisdom and knowledge, for whatever reason you enable us to love one another and trust you—for whatever reason, help us accept your truth as *our* truth.

O Lord, convince our minds that there *is* hope; that, with you, all things can be made new. Convince our spirits that there *is* faith; that, with you, all things can be made right. Convince our hearts that there *is* love; that, with you, all things can be made one. Convince us, and faith, hope, and love will abide. Convince us, and love shall prevail, the greatest and strongest of them all.[85]

Benediction. O God of beginnings, encourage our hearts as we greet this new hour, this new day, this new year! Knit us gently together in love, so that when we go apart in body, we shall be one in spirit.

---

[85] Inspired by I Corinthians 13.

Epiphany

Lections: Isaiah 60:1-6; Psalm 72:1-14; Ephesians 3:1-12; Matthew 2:1-12

Call to Worship

L: Lift up your eyes, O lands of the earth!
    For the star of the Lord has burst through the night!
P: We shall lift up our eyes to follow its path;
    we shall take up our staffs to embark on our journey.
L: Arise, shine; for your light has come! The glory of heaven
    has risen upon you!
P: We shall see and be radiant; we shall thrill and rejoice—
A: For this star shall dance over the cradle of God!

Invocation. O Lord, we have come. Come, now, to us. Send upon us your Grace, for you have called us to be its stewards. Speak to us your Word, for you have summoned us to be its witnesses. Show us your Body, for you have made us to be its members. Let the working of your power be seen among us, O God, that our works might declare your presence among the nations.

Litany

L: The Lord our God has sent our Savior!
    The face of God shines among the peoples!
P: O heaven and earth, raise glory to God!
    O mountains, echo the praise of the prairies!
L: For our Savior shall live longer than the moon, beyond
    the sun, through all generations!
P: O showers, fall and sweeten the grass!
    O wastelands, flower; and deserts, bloom!
L: For our Savior shall hear the sigh of the orphan, the cry of
    the outcast, throughout the ages!
P: From sea to sea, to the ends of the earth,
    the peoples gather to behold the Lord!
L: For justice rides on the Savior's shoulder, and righteous-
    ness strides on the Savior's heel!

A: "Joy to the world, the Lord is come! Let heaven and nature sing!"[86]

Prayer for One Voice. O God of wisdom, your voice calls to us as we wander. It thunders in the storms of the nightfall; it sighs in the mists of the morning. It laughs in the leaves at twilight; it sings with the sparrows at dawn.

Your voice falls on the hearts of all who will hear. You do not bequeath to some the privilege of your presence and to others the poverty of your absence. Whether we be rich or poor, weak or strong, fool or sage, your voice speaks to us. And where your voice is heard, the Word is born, and through the Word all things are made new.

All things shall be made new. This is your promise to creation, and what better sign of that promise than a rainbow arising in the midst of the rain, or a birth arriving in the midst of pain. But so often when you set your bow in the sky, we fail to see it, for our eyes are bound to the earth. And too often when you send new life from the womb, we fail to love it, for our hearts are bound to the past.

It is true, Lord. Sometimes we do not welcome what is new. Broken, we do not want an in-breaking. We want to shut our doors against the world when you would have us throw them open and make the world our home. We want to clutch our treasures to our breasts when you would have us go on a pilgrimage to place them in another's hands. We want to repeat our favorite proverbs when you would have us keep silent and kneel at the sound of a baby's cry.

The wise ones kneel before the Child, O God, but Herod plots to kill him. What shall we do, Lord? Who are we that you are mindful of us, that you send the Child to save us?

O Lord of the Magi, help us be wise, but not in the ways of *this* world. Let us not, like Herod, try to destroy the new; lest we, like Herod, seek to silence the Word.

Benediction. Radiant God, we have followed your star over

---

[86] From the hymn "Joy to the World" by Isaac Watts.

"field and fountain, moor and mountain,"[87] traveling far to find you. With great joy we have offered you our gifts. And, receiving them, you have lavished upon us the unsearchable riches of Christ. Now, having knelt before you, let us not return to Herod, but let us depart to our homes by a new way.

Human Relations Day/Martin Luther King, Jr., Day

Lections: Isaiah 42:1-7; Psalm 78:1-4, 12-17; James 2:5-9, 12-17; Matthew 10:34-42

Call to Worship
L: As the Lord parted the waters of the sea, the Lord breaks down the middle walls of partition,
P: To deliver us from the prejudices that divide and to lead us to the riches that unite.
L: As the Lord called prophets in times past, the Lord calls prophets in our time,
P: To sound the call for justice and to light the path to peace.
L: As the Lord sought disciples for yesterday's prophets, the Lord seeks disciples for today's prophets.
A: Here we are, Lord! Send us!

Invocation. O God of the one family of humanity, who seeks to bind us together on earth as in heaven, we gather now to ponder the implications of this quest for us human beings. We have come to pay tribute to those who count life a small price to pay for this unity. We have come not to deny the frailty of their humanity, but to affirm the clarity of their vision; not to question the imperfection of their judgment, but to acknowledge the beauty of their courage. We have also come to remind ourselves that the task to which you call them and us is as yet unfinished. As we take our place in the struggle for the beloved community, grant us, O Lord, the same willingness to risk and determination to triumph that drove those on whose shoulders we stand.

---

[87] From the hymn "We Three Kings" by John H. Hopkins.

Litany

L: O God, who through today's prophets delights our nameless nobodies and confounds our notable some-bodies, we honor them for all they do to make human relations truly human.

P: We thank you, dear Lord, for their noble life and courageous faith.

L: For their ability to walk in the shoes of the oppressed, and their readiness to step on the toes of oppressors,

P: We thank you, dear Lord.

L: For their loyalty to the church passionate for justice, and their resistance to the church tolerant of injustice,

P: We thank you, dear Lord.

L: For their willingness to negotiate with church and state, and their readiness to appeal to a higher court,

P: We thank you, dear Lord.

L: For their vigor in challenging unjust laws, and their submission to the penalties for defying them,

P: We thank you, dear Lord.

L: For their indifference to the lure of position and possessions, and their love for people and principle,

P: We thank you, dear Lord.

A: The Promised Land is brought near by their noble life and courageous faith. O God, help us by *our* life and faith to bring it nearer still.

Prayer for One Voice. O God of all humanity, we are restless until we find our place in your family. For this we thank you, as we remember all those who have helped us in our search for this place. We adore you, dear Lord, for surrounding us with such caring brothers and sisters.

Time does not permit the roll call of all their names. But on this day, as a way of symbolizing both our debt to them and our appreciation for them, we single out the name of Martin Luther King, Jr. When we think of this man, we are moved to utter astonishment. We would be hard pressed to think of another person who has so quickly worked such radical changes in human society. Certainly life for persons of color and lovers of peace has not been the same after King as before. If their watchwords have become change and nonviolence—as they have, from Latin America to South Africa to Southeast Asia—much of the credit can be laid at the door of this man: this man who said things others dared not say; this man who did things others dared not do; this man who changed things others said could not be changed—this man, who convinced people not to accept a helpless tomorrow just because they had lived through a miserable yesterday. We thank you, dear Lord, for the life and work of Dr. King—a prophet of hope, an apostle of nonviolence, an agent of change, a prince of peace and, above all, a servant of God and humanity.

His works do not astonish us solely because of their magnitude. They astonish us because his contemporaries had such marvelous excuses for deferring the struggle. Sociologists said his goals were unrealistic. Politicians complained that he was pursuing them too fast. Preachers denounced them for being not only untimely but unwise.

To his credit, without claiming to be either better or wiser or more timely than his critics, King set his face steadfastly toward Memphis, even though he knew it could mean rebuke, suffering, and death. He refused all excuses for postponing until tomorrow the changes that are needed today. We thank you, dear Lord, for the gift of this leader, blessed with remarkable wisdom, exquisite timing, and eloquent courage, a courage that enabled him to put his critics and their excuses in their place.

As we recall his heroic battle for peace with justice, we are haunted by a deep sense of guilt. Not only do we remember the calls to join his cause that we never answered, we also remember the speed with which we embraced the excuses that he dismissed.

Let us not now betray him in death as we did in life. In this land and in others, in our day as in his, oppression is in the saddle and tyranny is on the throne; injustice is in the factories and hunger is on the march; the rich are getting richer and the homeless are getting the shaft; the racists are growing boastful and their victims are growing desperate. Save us, O God, from the temptation once again to leave the cause of justice to other hands. Deliver us, too, from relying solely on divine intervention for the achievement of justice. Let us not forget that divine intervention works best through human effort—that just as we look to you for guidance, you look to us for action.

Benediction. Almighty God, as you have drawn us together in honor of your prophets, send us forth to settle the Promised Land that they saw from the mountaintop but were not allowed to enter. Give us, as you gave them, tough minds and tender hearts, that we too might become apostles of nonviolence in a land of violence, champions of justice in a society of injustice, and heralds of peace in a world of conflict.

Festival of the Home/Intergenerational Celebration

Lections: Deuteronomy 26:5-11; Psalm 145:1-7; Ephesians 2:19-22; Luke 2:41-52

Call to Worship
L: Come, and be no longer strangers;
P: Come, let us end our wanderings.
L: Pilgrims, travel no longer alone,
P: But let us visit hidden places.
L: Come! No matter where you go, you shall always be at home:
P: For we are the dwelling place of our God!
L: Through all your days, God's cloud shall lead you;
P: Through all our nights, God's fire shall burn[88]:
A: Young and old, we shall see and know, and all the people shall praise the Lord!

Invocation. O God, we were far from home. We had squandered our inheritance; we had sinned against you; we were not worthy to be called your children.[89]

---

[88] Inspired by Exodus 40:38.
[89] See Luke 15:21.

But now, O God, we have come home. Where would we be but in our Father's house? Where would we learn but at our Mother's knee?

Let your Spirit dwell within us, Lord, so that when you seek us, you shall find us where you would have us be.

Litany

L: This is the story of our house,

P: As told by our grandmother, as told to our grandson:

L: We went down and sojourned in Egypt, and we were few in number.

P: But there we grew, and we became many; there we grew, and we became strong.

L: The Egyptians, watching our house increase, began to treat us harshly.

P: They laid their whips upon our backs and locked their irons upon our legs; they saw us and did not understand, they looked upon us and felt afraid.

L: So we cried to the Lord, the God of our parents,

P: "Bring peace to this house, give us our freedom—before brother strikes sister out of anger and mother bruises child out of despair!"

L: The Lord heard our voice, and saw our affliction:

P: How long we toiled, yet had nothing to eat; how hard we sweated, yet had nowhere to sleep.

L: The Lord saw, and the Lord delivered us from Egypt:

P: With a mighty hand and an outstretched arm, the Lord brought us into this place, a land flowing with milk and honey.

L: This is the story of the house of the Lord,

P: As told by our grandfather, as told to our granddaughter:

A: Let us hear with our hearts and understand, that all brothers might clasp the hand of their sisters and all parents might rise on behalf of their children.

Prayer for One Voice. O God in whom we dwell, O God who dwells within us, hear our prayer! This day we celebrate the home, the place that is more than just *a* place. This day we celebrate communion, the belonging that is more than just belonging *to*. This day we celebrate the generations, the lifetimes that are more than just times in our lives.

We celebrate, O Lord, but our celebration is sobered by the knowledge that all is not well among us. The home in which we rejoice has been built for all too few; the communion on which we depend has been broken for far too many; the generations whom we love have been forgotten all too often.

We know that it is not good to be alone, but it can be so hard to stay together. So teach us how better to talk to one another, to listen to one another, to confront and affirm one another; teach us, Lord, how better to respect and love one another. Like the child Jesus, tarrying in the Temple when his parents thought he was trudging home, persons are not always where we believe them to be. We believe them to be well, but they are wounded; to be at peace, but they are troubled; to be stable, but they are insecure. The young we assume to be foolish, then they startle us with their wisdom; to be preoccupied, then they surprise us with their sensitivity. The old we assume to be settled, then they amaze us with their daring; to be distracted, then they astound us with their ingenuity.

We go to bed one night, and we awaken in the morning to find that our children are far beyond us, sitting among their teachers, listening astutely, asking sharp questions that even we do not understand. One day we leave our parents, and the next we knock on their door and stand, face to face, like strangers staring at someone who looks familiar but whose name escapes us. We do not understand; we can only ponder these things in our hearts.

All is not well, O Lord, but you promise that it can be better. So we give thanks for the glimpses of your presence in our home and in those who dwell therein. We hope for the day when the glimpse shall be a vision; and the vision, a reality; and the reality, your kingdom. For on that day you shall pour out your Spirit upon all flesh, and our sons and our daughters shall prophesy; our youths shall see visions, and our elders shall dream dreams; on all men and women you shall pour out your Spirit, and *all* will prophesy![90] On that day

---

[90] See Acts 2:17-18.

we shall see you on earth, *your* home, the place that is more than just *a* place. On that day we shall join you in communion, *your* communion, the belonging that is more than just a belonging *to*. On that day we shall embrace you for all generations, *your* generations, the lifetimes that are more than just times in our lives. For you, O God, shall lift us into eternity, and there we shall behold one another in all fullness, there where your dominion endures forever.

Benediction. We sang your praises, Lord, and as our voices mingled, our elders became youths, and our youths became elders. You are the One who embraces all generations, who makes of us together more than we can make of ourselves alone. Every day we will bless you for this, O God, that the world may witness the faithfulness of your word and the graciousness of your work.

Peace with Justice Sunday/World Communion Sunday/ Christian Unity

Lections: Isaiah 25:6-9; Psalm 34:1-3, 15-22; Revelation 7:9-17; Luke 24:13-28

Call to Worship
L: O come, let us make a joyful noise unto the Lord, the Creator of us all,
P: Who makes of one blood all the peoples of the earth!
L: O come, let us make a joyful noise unto the Lord, the Redeemer of us all,
P: Who makes all peoples one that we might seek and find the Lord!
L: O come, let us make a joyful noise unto the Lord, the Sustainer of us all,
P: Who makes all peoples one that we might know and serve the Lord!
A: O come, let us praise the Lord, our creator, redeemer and sustainer!

Invocation. O God of all peoples, your prophets foresaw a day when your Messiah would shatter the barriers between all nations and host a banquet for all peoples in celebration of the defeat of death, the triumph of joy, and the end to human separation. We gather in the name of the one who left us with a Holy Communion to symbolize that vision and a Holy Community to realize it. Let our observance of communion in this community hasten the fulfillment of your promise to the prophets.

Litany
L: Let us pray for the coming of the reign of the Lord,
P: That the Lord's will be done on earth as in heaven.
L: Lead us from temptation and deliver us from evil;
P: Let your will be done on earth as in heaven!
L: Give the hungry to eat and the thirsty to drink;
P: Let your will be done on earth as in heaven!
L: Lift up the despondent and wipe away their tears;
P: Let your will be done on earth as in heaven!
L: Rend the veil between castes and creeds;
P: Let your will be done on earth as in heaven!
L: Spread a feast for all tribes and tongues;
P: On earth as in heaven, let them sing—
A: Let us sing with one voice, "Salvation belongs to our God!"

Prayer for One Voice. O God, in the body and blood of Jesus you gave us a vivid reminder of the hard demands of your justice and the limitless reaches of your grace. As we partake of this sacrament, we ask for deliverance from all the parochial concerns that disrupt the universal fellowship for which you made and redeemed us. Help us look beyond the elements of our communion to the dimensions of our commitment, beyond our ceremony to our responsibility. Let us consider the life of the One in whose memory we join in this meal—how he elevated concern for persons above concern for programs; how he subordinated the practice of piety to acts of mercy; how he cast aside centuries-old prejudices to make redemption as inclusive as creation. Reflecting on this one life, we can only thank you, dear Lord, for this sacrament—for its assurance of communion with you and with the world.

Forgive us, O God, when our nation resists your summons to global communion. We have raised barriers between ourselves and others, and we have let stand barriers that we could have lowered. We have been less than even-handed in our international relations; our concern for justice has not always dictated our offers of assistance. Often, too often for our good and the good of others, we as a nation have failed you.

We have also failed you as individuals. We have not done enough to steer the ship of state into the path of peace with justice. So we ask, dear Lord, that you take away our guilt. Awaken our conscience! Restore our integrity! Make us restless until we cease regretting our sins and begin to redress them; until our words of remorse are matched by deeds of service; until we have realized our responsibility for human welfare and globalized our commitment to human rights.

O Lord, we regret the absence from your table of those who have broken communion with us. Help us all to see that this table is not theirs, or ours, but yours. Let us not, in the midst of our differences, mistake our pride for purity, or our stubbornness for saintliness. Let us, instead, leave judgment to you, for you alone can separate the wheat from the chaff, the saints from the sinners.

O God, whose heart grieves for those who are oppressed without relief, exploited without mercy, and mocked without pause, we commend these victims to your care. Aware that your intervention can come through our action, we pray that you will enlist us in the front lines of the struggle for justice. We come to your table to be forgiven for the battles behind us and to be fortified for the battles ahead of us. Our strength will be equal to the challenge only if you bless us with your presence. Without you, there is no battle we can win; with you, there is no enemy that we cannot defeat. So we ask you, O Lord, not to take our side, but to help us take yours.

CELEBRATION OF SPECIAL OCCASIONS

Benediction. O God, as you have brought us together to affirm our oneness in Christ, send us forth to proclaim our oneness in creation. As we have shared our Lord's Supper in worship, let us share our Lord's life in the world.

Memorial Day/All Saints Day

Lections: Wisdom of Solomon 3:1-9; Psalm 24; Revelation 21:1-6*a*; John 11:32-44

Call to Worship
L: Thus saith the Lord: That which is dead shall live again!
P: O Lazarus-man, come out from your tomb!
L: That which is sleeping shall rise again!
P: O Lazarus-brother, come out!
L: That which is broken shall be whole again!
P: O Lazarus-people, come out from your tomb!
L: I *am* resurrection; *I* am life![91]
P: O Lazarus-world, throw off your shroud!
     Take up your bed and walk!

Invocation. O God, this earth is yours in all its fullness, this world and all who dwell therein, for you are its creator, its father and mother; you, O Lord, are its life.

So who shall dare to ascend the mountain and meet you face to face?[92] And who shall stand in your holy place, where bushes burn and are not consumed?[93]

We are not worthy, Lord, but we shall dare as others have dared. We are not upright, but we shall stand as others have stood. We shall dare because we trust you, and we shall stand because we love you.

Litany
L: Let us remember those gone before,
P: Whose souls are in the hands of God,

---

[91] Inspired by John 11:25.
[92] See Exodus 19.
[93] Inspired by Exodus 3:2.

191

A: Where torment shall never touch them.
L: In the eyes of fools they seem to have died;
P: In the eyes of sages they appear in glory.
L: In the minds of fools their death was destruction;
P: In the minds of sages, transformation.
L: They were embattled;
P: They are at peace.
L: They were fatigued;
P: They are at rest.
L: They were distressed;
P: They are at ease.
L: They were alone;
P: They are one with God.
L: In life they fought their own mortality;
P: In death they yield to immortality.
L: In life they dimmed, their bodies tarnished;
P: In death they shine, their spirits burnished.
L: Like gold in a furnace they were tried and tested;
P: Like gold in a wheat field they reached the harvest.
L: Yes, let us remember those gone before,
P: Whose souls are in the hands of God,
A: Where torment shall never touch them.

Prayer for One Voice. O God, we call ourselves the resurrection people. Yet often we seem more the companions of death, more the friends of loss than of life. We love one another, then we leave one another. But, as the joy of loving increases, so does the pain of parting.

They say that parting is such sweet sorrow, Lord. But so often our sorrow is bitter, filled with so many regrets. So often our sorrow is angry, filled with so many questions. So often our sorrow is afraid, filled with so many doubts.

If parting be so sweet, Lord, why do we fall at your feet and cry, "Lord, if you had been here, our beloved would not have died!" Why does our heart lament, "If only we had done something more, if only we had said something sooner—?" Why does our heart argue, "What did she do to deserve this, why was he taken so soon—?" Why does our heart stare at the curve of a cheek, the back of a hand, the twinkle of an eye that has passed beyond our seeing?

If parting be so sweet, Lord, why do we beg you not to roll the stone away from the tomb? "By this time there will be an odor," we warn. "Our beloved has been dead for days." Though you remind us that soon we will see the glory of God, our eyes are fixed on the grave. It is not that we do not believe, Lord; it is that we do not believe with all our minds and all our hearts when confused by grief and pain.

Help us believe fully, O God. Bid Lazarus to stride forth, command our loved ones to walk out from their tombs; we shall embrace them, and then we will let them go. We will make peace with their peace, and find rest in their rest, and free them unto their freedom. They have sought your face, and they bask in its light; we see it shining, we see them shining, and not from afar. They are within us, with you, strengthening us with all power, according to your glorious might.

If parting be such sweet sorrow, Lord, we taste its sweetness only in such a vision as this, only in such a vision as revealed by you, our Maker, Redeemer, and Comforter.

Benediction. Be filled with all spiritual wisdom, that you may bear good fruit in your labor. Be strengthened with all spiritual power, that you may endure with patience and joy. Be blessed with all spiritual affection, that you may dwell with the saints who abide in the light, being delivered from the realm of the night into the glorious dominion of the sun.

Homecoming Sunday

Lections: Genesis 32:3-7a; 33:1-4, 8-11; Psalm 126; Hebrews 11:32-12:2; John 15:1-11

Call to Worship
L: Are we in a dream, we who stand in the light of day?
P: Our mouths are filled with laughter, our tongues with shouts of joy. The light we see is not of day: it streams from the face of God.

L: We came a great distance, and we were afraid;
P: As sinners we came home, and we feared the hand of the Lord.
L: But God has hurried to greet us; like Esau, the Lord has run out to meet us.
P: So let us embrace and weep together, let us confess our shame and our joy:
A: O, let us make merry and be glad together, for we who were dead are yet alive; we who were lost are found.[94]

Invocation. O God, apart from you we can do nothing; *with* you all things are already accomplished. We are only the branches, but abiding in the vine we bear good fruit. Abiding in one another, we abide in Christ; abiding in Christ, we abide in you.

O Tender of the Vine and Keeper of Life, abide with us. Let your joy be found in us, that our joy may be found in one another.

Litany
L: O prophets of God, you who are not acceptable in your own lands,[95] may you find peace among us.
P: You who through faith, not hate, conquer kingdoms of terror; you who through faith, not violence, raise justice to life; you who through faith, not death, stop the mouths of the lions; you who through faith, not fear, escape the edge of the sword—
A: You who are prophets of God, come home!
L: You who are not acceptable in your own lands, may you find peace among us.
P: If you have been mocked, we shall sing your praises; if you have worn chains, we shall break their memory; if you have been penniless, we shall give you treasure; if you have gone naked, we shall robe you in scarlet.
A: You who are prophets of God, come home!

---

[94] Inspired by Luke 15:32.
[95] Inspired by Luke 4:24.

L: You who are not acceptable in your own lands, may you find peace among us.

P: You of whom our world is not worthy, may you find us acceptable in your sight.

A: Without you we do not know ourselves, and without us you cannot be made whole. You are the Christ we crucified, and we are the people Christ came to save!

Prayer for One Voice. O God, we return to one another this day, and we return to you. We return to you like the prodigal come home—like Jacob come home to Esau, a trickster skulking back to the scene of his misdeed, confessing he is unworthy of the love being shown him. Like Jacob we come home, having prepared for you a great present of our ewes and rams, our camels and colts, our cows and bulls[96]—thinking, "We shall appease our God with the present that goes before us."[97]

But like Esau, O God, your concern is not with pacification but conciliation. Like Esau, you exclaim, "What do you mean by all this? I have plenty; keep what you have for yourself." Like Esau, you embrace us with the question, "Why do you bring me great treasure, when all I desire is you?" So you welcome us home—even though we have usurped our brother's place and stolen our sister's blessing.

You welcome us home as if we were your beloved prophets, with whom you are well pleased[98]; yet we are the killers of the prophets and the crucifiers of the Christ. How you love us! Your love is not earned; let us abandon all claims of worthiness. Your love is not manipulated; let us surrender all professions of faithfulness. Your love is not limited; let us banish all thoughts of hopelessness. Your love is not equaled; let us relinquish all feelings of helplessness.

Yours is a love that we need and admire, but which we rarely share. We are the brothers and sisters of Jacob; we are practiced at trickery. So remind us, O God, that we are also

---

[96] See Genesis 32:13-15.
[97] Inspired by Genesis 32:20.
[98] See Luke 3:22.

the brothers and sisters of Esau; we may not be saints, but we can rise above our sin to embrace a fellow sinner.

Bring us home, Lord. Bring us to an understanding of ourselves, of one another, and of you. When we next go apart, let it be not to flee but to travel the road to another reunion.

Benediction. Let us run to greet those who long to come home. And let compassion so light our way that they shall embrace us with gladness and sigh, "Truly, to see your face is to see the face of God, with such grace you have received us."

A National Observance

Lections: Jeremiah 22:13-19; Psalm 72:1-4, 12-14, 18-19; Philemon 1-3, 8-16; Matthew 22:15-22

Call to Worship
L: O come, let us sing to the Lord,
P: Let us sing a song of justice for this and every nation.
L: O come, let us sing to the Lord,
P: Let us sing a song of peace for this and every land.
L: O come, let us sing to the Lord,
P: Let us sing a song of love for this and every people.
A: O come, let us sing to the Lord, the God of all creation.

Invocation. O God of all nations, we approach you out of gratitude and concern for *our* nation. As we reflect on its achievements, we are grateful that its heritage has become ours. We are grateful, too, for all who have labored to shape it to your will.

Yet our gratitude for this heritage is matched by our concern for its perils. Pilot us, O God, through the treacherous waters, that we might do as well by our descendants as our ancestors did by us.

We boast of being "one nation under God." Help us, O Lord, to turn this proud claim into a true confession.

Litany

L: O Lord, who has given us the power to form our government,

P: Help us choose leaders of good ability and sound character.

L: From persons with a keener interest in mansions for themselves than homes for the poor,

P: Good Lord, deliver us.

L: From persons with a greater empathy for the dealers in oppression than the victims of exploitation,

P: Good Lord, deliver us.

L: From persons with a deeper fear of the prospects of change than the effects of injustice,

P: Good Lord, deliver us.

L: To persons with wills firm enough to persevere and considerate enough to be patient,

P: Good Lord, lead us.

L: To persons with hearts vulnerable enough to care and wise enough to be discreet,

P: Good Lord, lead us.

L: To persons with minds tough enough to inspire and tender enough to be responsive,

P: Good Lord, lead us.

A: Help us, dear Lord, so to form our government that it shall fulfill the promise of liberty and justice for all.

Prayer for One Voice. O Lord of all lands and nations, we thank you for allowing us to establish a nation in this land. When we think of this land, we are moved to awe by its size and beauty; and when we think of this nation, we are moved to gratitude for its founders and ideals. We are tempted to exclaim, "Would that every land could have such a nation, and that every nation could have such a land!"

Since this cannot be, we could reprove you for short-changing so many peoples. Or we could applaud you for playing favorites with us. Or we could extol you for so richly blessing us, and humbly ask for your guidance in meeting the challenge presented by such an incredible and undeserved gift. Of these options, we choose the last. So we thank you for the chance at life in such a nation in such a land, and we pray for your counsel in facing our responsibility.

Yet we cannot ask for more counsel without bemoaning our disregard of that we have already received. Repeatedly we have been told that we cannot endure the awful divisions that plague the world—a third rich and a third poor, a third highly educated and a third illiterate, a third well-housed and a third homeless. Despite these warnings, we have run one red light after another. We have squandered numerous opportunities for reducing the incidence of poverty-stricken, drug-addicted, and crime-infested neighborhoods. Wringing our hands and chanting our laments, we have simply waited for others to work the changes for which we called. We have boasted of having a government of, by, and for the people, yet we have been too preoccupied with securing special privileges for ourselves to contend for the basic rights of others.

Awaken us, O God, to our narrowness of vision and hardness of heart. Arouse us to our oneness with all humanity; when we appeal to those in authority over us, let us not forget those in misery below us. Make us zealous contenders for the ideals expressed in our founding documents: at patriotic celebrations, to be sure; but also in the places where change is conceived and born and nourished and brought to glorious flower in the triumph of justice—around the family table, in the classroom, in the board room, in the marketplace, and, yes, in the streets. This brand of zeal has rarely been our trademark, but this admission of failure will be of no consequence unless it be followed by deeds of penitence. So we ask you, dear Lord, for help. Restore to us, who are quick to denounce injustice against ourselves, the will to secure justice for others.

O Creator of us all, teach us to respect the people of other nations—for loving their land as we love ours; for supporting their government as we support ours; and for regarding their leaders as we regard ours. Give us the decency never to rejoice over the failure or fall of any nation—until, at the same time, we can pray for its transformation into a crusader for peace with justice.

O Lord, you have placed us in an imperfect nation and an imperfect world of constant change. Give us the vision to see the changes we should make, the strength to resist the changes we should not make, and the insight to distinguish the changes that will do us good from those that will do us harm. And let us, above all, be quick to seek and welcome allies in this earthly struggle for your heavenly will.

Benediction. O God, as here we have expressed gratitude for our nation's ideals, let us go forth to praise them in speech, codify them in law, and translate them into deed. As they turn our eyes from the successful to the struggling, give us the grace to remember that these ideals did not come to us without price, and will not survive without sacrifice.

Labor Day

Lections: Ecclesiastes 3:1, 9-13; Psalm 90:1-2, 16-17; Romans 12:3-8; Matthew 6:19-24

Call to Worship
L: O come, let us praise the Lord, who seeks a place for every worker under heaven—
P: A place for labor, and a place for leisure.
L: O come, let us praise the Lord, who seeks a place for every worker under heaven—
P: A place for self, and a place for service.
L: O come, let us praise the Lord, who seeks a place for every worker under heaven—
P: A place for planning, and a place for prayer.
A: O come, let us praise the Lord, the God of all workers in every place!

Invocation. O Christ, Master Worker of the ages, lead us to the architect of your design for life. Let us study the elements of this masterpiece until they become elements of our own design: the heart that sacrifices personal gain for social good; the mind that considers long-term consequences as well as short-term costs; and the conscience that spurns evil, regardless of the consequences. Clarify your design for our labor, O Lord, that our life may become worthy of the foundation you laid.

Litany

L: As in the Christian community we have many members but serve different functions, so it is in the human community,

P: And all its members, despite their diversity of functions, are nevertheless one.

L: Therefore, let us not think of ourselves too highly or of our neighbors too lowly,

P: But let us think with sober judgment, remembering that the only function we have in common is to serve the common good.

L: Having functions that differ, if our work is on the assembly line,

P: Let us see to it that our factory serves the common good.

L: Having functions that differ, if our work is in the hospital,

P: Let us see to it that our medicine serves the common good.

L: Having functions that differ, if our work is on a janitorial staff,

P: Let us see to it that our housekeeping serves the common good.

L: Having functions that differ, if our work is in the classroom,

P: Let us see to it that our teaching serves the common good.

L: Having functions that differ, if our work is on the farm,

P: Let us see to it that our farming serves the common good.

L: Having functions that differ, if our work is in the courtroom,

P: Let us see to it that the law serves the common good.

L: Having functions that differ, no matter where or what
    our work may be,
A: Let us see to it that our work serves the common good.

Prayer for One Voice. O God, the greatness and beauty of
whose work surrounds us from daybreak to sunset, let us
pause to reflect on the message you daily proclaim through
nature. Let her variety, her beauty, her productivity, and her
vulnerability tell us of her readiness to care for us and of our
need to care for her.

As you have populated the earth with different peoples,
you have blessed the earth's different regions with different
fruits and vegetables and animals. And as you have blessed
the earth with a variety of natural resources, you have
blessed your creatures with a diversity of skills. You have
indeed given us the raw materials for producing enough for
everybody's needs and skills enough to distribute them.

As we behold your creation and the way that you have
shaped it for our benefit, we can only marvel at the contrast
between your work and ours. Whereas your work spotlights
our interdependence, ours exaggerates our independence.
Whereas your work accents the need for mutual concern,
ours reflects a passion for self-interest. Whereas your work
trumpets the virtue of cooperation, ours glorifies the value of
competition.

O God, help us rediscover the ties that bind us in a
common family. Correct our distorted vision and corrupted
faith so that, instead of regarding unique abilities as grounds
for separation, we will recognize them as gifts for the
community; so that, instead of regarding education as a
license for special privilege, we will recognize it as a passport
to special responsibility; so that, instead of regarding
differences as excuses for conflict, we will recognize them as
instruments of peace; and so that, instead of regarding work
as a job to be endured, we will recognize it as a calling to be
embraced.

O God, who seeks to unite us in our love for you and one
another, teach us that we cannot serve two masters, one in
work and another in worship. Let the two become one, our

work giving expression to our worship, and our worship giving direction to our work.

Deliver us from the elitist impulse to judge others by the size of their income, the prestige of their position, or the nature of their work. Let us respect equally the work of the hands and the work of the mind. And help us remember that it is not the hands or the mind but the heart that is the measure of faithful labor.

Benediction. Eternal God, you have made us co-laborers with you in a good but imperfect world, in a formed but changing universe, in a healthy but precarious environment, and in a growing but dangerous society. As you send us forth to do your work, make us aware of the dangers and the opportunities of our task. Give us the patience of those who, without your blessing, would undertake nothing, and the impatience of those who, with your blessing, would undertake anything.

Thanksgiving

Lections: Joel 2:21-27; Psalm 126; I Timothy 2:1-7; Matthew 6:25-33

Call to Worship
L: Be glad, and rejoice!
P: The Lord has done great things!
L: Wilderness sands have become green pastures;
P: Barren trees have yielded good fruit.
L: Bitter grapes have turned sweet on the vine;
P: Empty vats are brimming with oil.
L: The birds of the air are feasting on manna;
P: The lilies of the field are robed in white.[99]
L: Yes, be glad and rejoice, O people of God!
A: The Lord is doing great things!

---

[99] Inspired by Revelation 7:9.

Invocation. This day, O Lord, we are like those who dream. For so long we have sown tears, for so long we have scattered the seeds of weeping. But this day, O God, you have restored us. This day we have harvested not hurt, but healing; this day we have reaped not rage, but redemption.

So hear us! We are coming home, bringing you sheaves of grain. Oh, run to us with open arms, that we might embrace you with gladness![100]

Litany

L: Fear not, O Land:

P: The Lord our God is great!

L: In the beginning God created two great lights, the sun to rule the day, and the moon to rule the night.[101]

P: And we who sat in darkness have seen; in the shadow of death the light has dawned.[102] Rejoice and be glad! The Lord our God is great!

L: Fear not, O Land:

P: The Lord has done great things!

L: An angel appeared in a great flame of fire in the midst of a bush; we looked, and the bush was burning, and yet was not consumed.[103]

P: We who sat in darkness have seen; in the shadow of death the light has dawned. Rejoice and be glad! The Lord has done great things!

L: Fear not, O Land:

P: The Lord is doing great things for us!

L: The angel of the Lord appeared, and the glory of the Lord shone all around. But the angel said, "Be not afraid; for behold, I bring you good news of a great joy which will come to all the people."[104]

---

[100] Inspired by Luke 15:20.
[101] Inspired by Genesis 1:16.
[102] Inspired by Matthew 4:16.
[103] Inspired by Exodus 3:2-3.
[104] Inspired by Luke 2:10.

P: We who sat in darkness have seen; in the shadow of death the light has dawned. Rejoice and be glad! The Lord is doing great things for us!

L: Fear not, O Land:

P: The Lord will do great things for all!

L: The day of Pentecost had come. And suddenly we heard a great sound from heaven like the rush of a mighty wind, and tongues of fire seemed to rest upon us all.[105]

P: We who sat in darkness have seen; in the shadow of death the light has dawned. Rejoice and be glad! The Lord will do great things for all!

Prayer for One Voice. O God, you are the Creator whose glorious light shines through the deepest of nights and darkest of days. You are the Proclaimer whose burning word speaks in the most common of places and routine of times. You are the Savior whose brilliant herald appears to the most simple of mortals and scorned of souls. You are the Inspirer whose fiery spirit rests upon the most fearful of disciples and feeble of wills.

You, O God, take the deep and the dark, the common and the routine, the simple and the scorned, the fearful and the feeble; you take *us,* and you say, "Do not be afraid. Do not be anxious. For which of you by being anxious can add one inch to your span of life?"

You take our world, and our deep becomes the depth of faith; our dark becomes that for which stars must be made; our common becomes the common good; our routine becomes that on which the rare must depend; our simplicity becomes the simplicity of spirit; our scorn becomes that from which love must be saved; our fear becomes the fear of the Lord; our feebleness becomes that from which strength must be born.

Take us, O God! If it be your desire that all should be saved, save us! We offer you supplications and prayers, intercessions and thanksgivings, and not for ourselves alone. We pray on behalf of all that is, of all who are; we pray for all that

---

[105] Inspired by Acts 2:1-14.

is worthy of praise, for all who praise you. We pray, not out of desperation but in celebration. We pray, not anxious about whispers that may go unanswered but in the assurance of promises fulfilled. We pray, for we cannot *not* pray. We pray to you, for we cannot be alone.

The birds of the air feast on manna; they eat, for they are not alone. The lilies of the field don robes of white; they are clothed, for they are not alone. The beasts of the pasture sleep on beds of green; they are at rest, for they are not alone. The seeds in the soil drink the showers of rain; they are alive, for they are not alone.

And we, the children of the Lord, are glad! For like the birds, we have no hunger that your presence will not satisfy; like the lilies, we have no nakedness that your presence will not clothe; like the beasts, we have no restlessness that your presence will not calm; and like the seed, we have no sleep that your presence will not awaken.

O Creator, we adore the glorious light that feeds the world; may all be filled. O Proclaimer, we praise the burning word that clothes the world; may all be protected. O Savior, we give thanks to the brilliant herald that calms the world; may all find peace. O Inspirer, we worship the fiery spirit that awakens the world; may all be changed, now and forever more.

Benediction. Let us go forth singing, bearing seed for sowing, that the children of God may return joyfully home, bringing in the sheaves.

Student Day

Lections: Deuteronomy 6:4-9, 20-25; Psalm 78:1-8; II Timothy 3:14-4:5; Matthew 11:25-30

Call to Worship
L: Come to me, all who labor and are heavy laden, and I will give you rest.
P: Our shoulders sag beneath the weight of the world, our

bodies bear the scars of its lessons. Let your presence fall upon us!

A: O Lord our God, please give us rest.[106]

L: Come to me, and learn from me, for I am gentle and lowly in heart.

P: Speak to us as to little children, that our shoulders might straighten and our bodies heal. Let your presence fall upon us!

A: O Lord our God, please give us your rest.

Invocation. O Lord of heaven and earth, you have hidden yourself from the wise and revealed yourself to babes. In the words of Jesus, "Such is your gracious will."

How we are humbled! We who idolize the wisdom of mature minds, *we* must look to the children. Playing among them, perhaps we can learn that what our intellects know is nothing compared to the rapture of being known; that what our minds accept is nothing compared to the joy of being accepted.

Come to us as to the children, Lord, and we shall sit at your feet, as we sit at theirs.

Litany

L: People of God, give ear to my teaching; incline your hearts to the words of my mouth.

P: Open your mouth in a parable; utter to us the mysteries of old.

L: Shall you hide my truths from your children and douse the fire that burns in their minds?

P: No, the children shall rise and be our teachers; they shall strike a spark in the caves of *our* minds.

L: Then kneel and watch them; learn from them with all your heart:

P: They shall leap to their feet and dance, to show us what has gone unseen.

---

[106] Inspired by Exodus 33:14.

L: Kneel and listen to them; learn from them with all your soul:

P: They shall stand in silence and sing with their hands, to tell us what has gone unheard.

L: Kneel and dream with them; learn from them with all your might:

P: They shall sit in a circle and spin great stories, to reveal to us what has never been.

L: For every stubborn and rebellious generation that dies, another generation shall be born—

P: And compassion can be its mother; faithfulness, its father.

L: For every heart that wavers and every spirit that wanders,

P: A heart can remain steadfast, and a spirit can come home.

L: I shall open my mouth in a parable, and utter through children the mysteries of old.

P: Let us give ear to your teaching and incline our hearts to the words of their youth!

Prayer for One Voice. O One through whom all knowledge is received, receive us, whose knowledge is so little! O One through whom all understanding is reached, reach out to us, whose understanding is so slight! O One through whom all wisdom comes, come to us, whose wisdom is so small!

An ancient one once admonished us, "You shall love the Lord your God with all your heart, and with all your soul, and with all your might. And these words shall be written upon your heart; and you shall teach them diligently to your children." We were not to utter these words to the little ones once and never again; we were to talk of them when we were sitting and walking, when we were lying down and rising up—we were to *live* them. Words inscribed on a page can be read, studied, memorized, even applied; but only words engraved upon the heart can be truly *lived,* and this was your desire.

But we, O God, have relied more upon the page than upon the heart, more upon what we could live *by* than upon what we could live *from*. And so, when the time came and our children asked, "What does all of this mean?" we had nothing to say. Though we had read and studied and memorized and even applied the words of the ancient ones, we had forgotten why we call ourselves your people; we had forgotten the old, old story.

"We were Pharaoh's slaves in Egypt," it went on, "and the Lord brought us out of Egypt with a mighty hand, and led us into the Promised Land."

Bondage and freedom, that was the story; captivity and release, that was the reason. But our memory of the chain being broken had faded, and now we were carrying its legacy only because it was the thing to do. Our remembrance of a heavy yoke being lifted had grown dull, and now we were passing on its tradition simply because it had always been done.

But change is at the beginning, the middle, and the end of the story, O God! Refresh our memory! Whisper into the ear of the child kicking in the womb, the child yet unborn, saying, "Arise, and speak my word to your parents, so that they may set their hope in me, and not forget my works; lest they pass away, a stubborn and rebellious generation, whose heart was not steadfast, whose spirit was not faithful."

Whisper into the ear of the child stretching for a star, the child becoming a youth, saying, "Be unfailing in patience and in teaching, for the time approaches when people will not endure your words, but, having itching ears, they will look for teachers to suit their own liking."

Whisper into the ear of the child witnessing the new age, the child becoming a prophet, saying, "As for you, always be steady, endure suffering, spread the gospel, fulfill your ministry."

O God, whisper unto them the secrets that you seek to share with us—secrets you would whisper to us, were it not for the roar in our ears of what we have so surely taught ourselves. Calm us, dear Lord, so that, if we cannot hear you, we can at least hear the children.

Benediction. I charge you in the presence of God and Jesus

Christ: learn with all your heart, for it is the page on which God's truth is written; serve with all your soul, for it is the arm by which God's strength is proven; and love with all your might, for it is the lamp by which God's way is taken.

Rural Life

Lections: Deuteronomy 11:8-17; Psalm 147:1-11; Romans 8:18-25; Mark 4:26-32

Call to Worship
L: To the outcast I say, "Come, in the name of the Lord!"
P: For the Lord shall gather us into a land that flows with milk and honey.
L: To the brokenhearted I say, "Come, in the name of the Lord!"
P: For the Lord shall heal us in a land that drinks from the cup of heaven.
L: To the downtrodden I say, "Come, in the name of the Lord!"
P: For the Lord shall guard you in a land that rises from seed to grain.
A: From the morning of planting 'til the evening of harvest, from the beginning of life 'til the end of time, come unto the Lord!

Invocation. O Lord, you take delight in the horse, that glorious beast sculpted by your hands; but you take greatest delight not in the strength of the charging steed but in the faith of those made strong in you. You find pleasure in the grain, that splendid seed sown by your hands; but you find greatest pleasure not in the fairness of the flowering fields but in the hope of those made fair in you.

O Lord, make us strong, and we shall fortify this earth with faith. Make us fair, and we shall beautify this earth with hope. Make us strong and fair, and we shall glorify this earth with love!

Litany
L: O Spirit of the silent night, who sprinkles the sky with glitter while we sleep and calls each star by name,

P: Hear the prayer of your people! Rouse us from our sleeping, awaken our eyes to the beauty of the cosmos! Lift the veil between earth and sky, reveal the suns of the universe! Then shall we see and know and support your sky on the pillars of our dreams.

L: O Spirit of the sacred day, who covers the heavens with clouds while we plant and then anoints the seed with rain,

P: Hear the prayer of your people! Sanctify us in our planting, hallow the ground to the glory of the harvest! Establish the root of the seed in good soil, feed its life with showers of blessing! Then shall we see and know, and carry your day on the shoulders of our toil.

L: O Spirit of the untamed creature, who gives the beast its food while we feast and tends the fledgling in the nest,

P: Hear the prayer of your people! Humble us in our feasting, bring all nature to partake of the banquet! Break bread for them and offer the cup, feed the wolf and the lamb together![107] Then shall we see and know, and protect your creatures with the staff of our life.

L: O Spirit of the Easter land, who cloaks the hills in green while we watch and summons the lily from its bud,

P: Hear the prayer of your people! Keep us constant in our watching, parade the seasons of paradise through our vigil! Raise the dead from the earth, breathe new breath into their being! Then shall we see and know, and lift your land on the wings of our joy.

Prayer for One Voice. O Lover of rolling hills and craggy mountains, of teeming forests and thriving plains, of tripping streams and thundering rivers, of soaring birds and lumbering beasts, of wild flowers and cultivated fields; O Lover of open and wind-swept places, of hidden and untouched spaces, of storm and sun, of seed and soil, of the mystery that makes and moves all that breathes upon this

---

[107] Inspired by Isaiah 11:6.

earth, and beyond this earth—O Lover of *us*, you are our God!

You are the God of hope, the God who sees something beyond what is. Your world is a world of change, whirling in motion. Creation does not despair; she aspires. She is not content with who she is; she anticipates what she can become. She rocks and moans, she groans in the throes of birth, and her present sufferings do not compare to the glory that shall be her children.

Her birth cry splits the air of the countryside, Lord. Her travail breaks the ground of the farmlands. Creation awaits her deliverance with eager longing, and it comes! Trees bud in her womb and bloom in spring and summer; then come autumn and winter—the blooms blush, and are blown away. Then creation, keeping the commandment given her, loving you and serving you with all her heart and soul, begins her labor once again.

We are her children, Lord, even as we are yours. But we are not so faithful to our destiny as creation is to hers. We turn aside and serve other gods; we follow messiahs who can release us from the divine cycle of birth and death and rebirth. We await our salvation with eager longing, but let it come from another god! We renounce Mother Earth and forsake you. We look with contempt upon nature and with scorn upon deity. And in our contempt we rape the land; in our scorn we defile your name.

Forgive us, Lord, for we have relinquished our hope in you. This day we reclaim that hope. This day we affirm the pattern you have established for our lives—for all life—and we attest to the goodness of all you have made.

Restore to us, O God, the faith that we have maimed, and help us restore the land that we have disfigured. Remake us in your image! And we too shall become lovers of open and windswept places, of hidden and untouched spaces, of storm and sun, of seed and soil, of the mystery that makes and moves all that breathes upon this earth, and beyond this earth, O God, our Messiah!

Benediction. Do not despair of what is seen, but hope for what is not seen. Do not abandon what is, but await what will be. Prepare the ground! For if you scatter the seed, it shall grow; you may not perceive it, you may not understand how such a tiny bit could crack through the crusty earth to smile at heaven. But do not fear; only plant the seed, and the small shall become mighty.

Urban Life

Lections: Jeremiah 29:1, 4-14; Psalm 107:1-9; Revelation 21:1-4; Luke 19:41-44

Call to Worship
L: Behold the holy city descending from heaven!
P: Cities of earth, behold your God!
L: We have cried to the Lord, and the Lord has heard;
P: We have sought the Lord, and the Lord is found.
L: Sing to the Lord, who builds a new city and gathers us in.
P: From east and west, we shout, "Hallelujah!" From north and south, we declare, "Amen!"
A: O, behold the new Jerusalem, come down from heaven with our God!

Invocation. We were wandering in the wastelands, in the swamps and the deserts; hungry and thirsty, our souls were faint. But you, O God, delivered us from our distress. You led us to a city in which to dwell, and where there was none, you gave us tools with which to build.

This day, O God, we seek the welfare of the city. This day, O God, we seek the things that make for peace. For our enemies have surrounded us, hemming us in on every side; they dash our children to the ground, and leave no brick standing upon another.

Lord, we call upon you in our time of trouble; hear us! We seek you with all our hearts; be found!

Litany
L: O Lord, we know that the plans you have for us are plans for good and not for evil,

P: For you are the God of hope, not despair; of expectation, not extinction.

L: We know you have helped us raise the city; yours is the arm that has gathered us in,

P: That we may build houses and live in them—

L: Plant gardens and eat from them—

P: Join hands and work with them—

L: Share minds and explore with them— ·

P: Discover crafts and create with them.

L: You have helped us raise the city; yours is the arm that has gathered us in:

P: You said, "Let there be a city," and so it was, and you saw that the city was good.

L: Therefore, we will not fear though the city should change,

P: Though its foundations should tremble and its walls should quake.[108]

L: No, we shall prepare for your visitation,

P: When the new Jerusalem shall come upon us in fulfillment of your promise.

L: If we call, you shall hear; if we seek, you shall be found.

P: We shall see a new heaven and a new earth coming down out of heaven, and all former things shall pass away.

A: Then the country shall be known as the Garden of Eden, with the tree of life at its center; and the city shall be called the City of God, with the tree of knowledge at its heart.[109]

Prayer for One Voice. Lord of heaven and of earth, of former things and future things, we call upon your name! Whenever your name is uttered, time stands still; wherever your name is uttered, space stretches forever. Yet here, at this moment and in this place, eternity seems not time enough and infinity seems not space enough to receive our prayer.

Our prayer is for the city, that terrible and wonderful place of our time. Terribly the city tempts us, not three times, but

---

[108] Inspired by Psalm 46:2.
[109] Inspired by Genesis 2:9.

thirty-times-three and seventy-times-seven.[110] How often we must be forgiven, and how often we must forgive! Terribly the city tests us, not once, but again; not in one way, but in all. How hard we are tried, and how hard we must try!

The city is our adversary, not to be ignored, neither to be forgotten. It is a strong and dangerous opponent, demanding recognition for what it is and compelling the respect due a foe. This is the city that has forgotten, even forbidden you, O God. This is where the Tower of Babel looms large, eclipsing even the light of heaven, the symbol of human pride and inhuman power.[111]

But, then, how the city can deliver us from smallness of vision and narrowness of concern. Wonderfully the city rescues us from the selfishness born of isolation and the stinginess sired by seclusion. How often are we redeemed, and how often we must redeem! Wonderfully the city liberates us, not once, but again; not in once way, but in all. How fiercely are we loved, and how fiercely we must love!

The city is our advocate, not to be ignored, neither to be forgotten. It is a powerful and passionate partisan, demanding recognition for what it is and compelling the respect due a champion. This is the city that has not forgotten, and never forbidden you, O God. This is where the tree of the cross looms tall, shedding even the light of heaven, the symbol of superhuman love and superhuman power.

O Lord, we pray for this, our city, in all its terror and wonder. May your eternity hold the city in its hand; may your infinity protect the city with its arm, until the day of the new Jerusalem.

Benediction. O God, look with compassion upon the city; wipe away every tear from its eyes, and banish death; exile its grief and pain to the desert, to perish there of thirst. O Lord, we cry out! Visit us! Let your new Jerusalem come, that you might look upon us without weeping and enter a city where every foot is leaping with joy on golden streets.

---

[110] Inspired by Matthew 18:21-22.
[111] Inspired by Genesis 12:1-9.

Index of Scriptural Passages

LITANIES AND OTHER PRAYERS

INDEX